"This book is glorious, not only for the recipes, but also the spectacu⸺ ⸺⸺ ⸺⸺y that conveys the spirit and the life of The Kitchen." Yvonne Grimbeek, *City Press*, 27 May 2012, p. 12

"*A Week in The Kitchen* has been resoundingly well received. Its success lies in the fruitful combination of Dudley's cuisine, clean design by Roxanne Spears of Good Design and Russel Wasserfall's many stunning full-page photographs, which give the impression of not being posed." Brent Meersman, *Mail&Guardian*, 11 May 2012, p. 9

"The unique vibe, quirky décor and down-to-earth goodness that comes from providing sustenance to an entire community daily is captured in the fun cookbook." *Shape* magazine, 1 July 2012, p. 66

"What Karen's wonderful book does for me (apart from sharing her delicious recipes) is to convey the humanity and homeliness of The Kitchen, both the people who work there and the people who visit to enjoy the food." Posted under *Cook Book Review, Spotlight* by Clare, www.spill.co.za, 10 May 2012

"It got nationwide attention when first lady Michelle Obama ate there last year. US embassy spokesperson Elizabeth Kennedy-Trudeau said 'We understand the first lady enjoyed the lunch tremendously.' Which isn't surprising, going by the gorgeous images and imaginative recipes in Dudley's book, *A Week in The Kitchen.*" Sue de Groot, *Sunday Times, Food Weekly*, 22 April 2012

"It's achieved almost cult status, not only because it's where the US First Lady Michelle Obama chose to stop for a bite on a visit to SA in 2011, but because of the sheer magic that owner Karen and her team create daily." *Shape* magazine, 1 July 2012, p. 66

"Karen shares her generous food philosophy and recipes in a new book, *A Week in The Kitchen.*" *ELLE*, 1 May 2012, p. 145

"It's not just a cook book, in fact it's so far from being a studio-styled culinary creation that I'm not sure what to call it. It's much more." Matt Allison, www.curatethisspace.com, 16 April 2012

"For those who cannot pass by the restaurant for a first-hand experience of the "love sandwich", be sure to acquire a copy of the book, for the next best thing…" Amy, jacana.bookslive.co.za, 25 April 2012

"*A Week in The Kitchen* is a celebration of Karen Dudley's eatery, The Kitchen, situated in the heart of Woodstock. The book, like the restaurant, radiates with the warmth and charm of its owner." Megan, www.wordsworth.co.za, 23 May 2012

"This book is a beautifully compiled daily account of the food and activity of a week in The Kitchen. It's a quirky combination of yummy recipes and 'fly-on-the-wall' photographs of the people who frequent the famous lunchtime spot in the funky little neighbourhood of Woodstock, Cape Town." Julie Taylor, Book of the month for June 2012, www.wine-style.co.za

A WEEK IN
The Kitchen

A WEEK IN
The Kitchen

KAREN DUDLEY

with Russel Wasserfall & Roxanne Spears

a few words

In my earliest days of school, our Sub A (Grade 1) teacher sent us home with a pile of books to be covered by our moms in regulation brown paper. My mom sent me back to school with the pile of exercise books covered in the brightest floral paper. The teacher looked with disdain at my books. "Tell your mother to cover these in brown paper!" I took them home again and explained how everyone else had brown paper covered books and would she please recover them according to the teacher's orders? My mother was adamant. Why should books be covered in brown paper when you are in Sub A? She sent them back still in their garish wrapping. I was never going to be like everyone else. I was to celebrate what was extraordinary.

The Kitchen is driven by these instincts:

Life is too short for the arbitrary, the mediocre, the "nice". If you are going to eat something, however simple, it must be all that it is meant to be. It must be essentially good.

Contrast, colour, a riot of flavour – this is the stuff we live by, this is the stuff we celebrate!

Food made with generosity and attention has the power to grow a community and to make people happy. There is reciprocity here. As we spend our love, so it comes back to us threefold.

This book has been cajoled into being by many friends of The Kitchen. This is the way we want to eat: a great selection of vegetables, fresh and good. These are the "Mains". The meat dishes are the "Accompaniment".

Every day in The Kitchen we make over 20 salads and loads of Treats and Love Sandwiches. It is my pleasure to offer many customers a little morsel of something that has just come out of the oven, or a Treat that has just been cut. *A Week in The Kitchen* is just such a sampling of all the food and activity that happened in a week in November 2011. It is with joy and pride that we offer you this book.

putting it together

We knew from the outset what we wanted to do: select some of the salads we make every week at The Kitchen and photograph the whole book over the course of one week. The book would develop in real time alongside the food! No studios, no extra lighting, and using only the props and linens already in The Kitchen!

We decided to have a celebratory lunch for the Sunday of our book, and I invited friends and family to my home in Woodstock. In the same way we cater parties we made food at The Kitchen for a party at home.

There were two main challenges in writing the book. One was recording the recipes we make daily that had not been written up but were so part of our currency. Annabel Healey, a human rights lawyer about to move to Ireland, was our first "intern". Annabel volunteered to spend two weeks with us in September and I tasked her with the business of extracting some of the unrecorded recipes of The Kitchen from the women who make them.

Since we make our salads in large quantities, I had to scale them down to recipes that would feed eight people. As I wrote the recipes, I had Sophie Fraser test each one to be sure of accuracy. Our goal was to make them as accessible as possible.

I also knew from the start that I wanted to make the book with Russel and Roxy. Roxy and Russel, who have been friends for years and have worked on a number of books together, took me into their creative unit. Together, shooting this book was exhilarating and inspiring. It cemented our affection for each other and our creative bond.

The people who make it all seem easy are really The Kitchen's kitchen crew. It will be hard to find a harder-working, more versatile and more talented team. Every day they put dishes together with grace and skill, ever multitasking and helping each other to seamlessly execute hundreds of tasks, filling the display fridge with our customary array of food and sending out party after party. It is their commitment and pride that are the real driving force behind The Kitchen experience.

My friend, artist and wordsmith, Peter van Straten, and my sweetheart, David Mallinson, read my script and encouraged me with their incisive input and wisdom.

contents

Monday   14

Tuesday   48

Wednesday   80

Thursday   114

Friday   144

Saturday   closed

Sunday   176

Kitchen Tips   212

List of Recipes   220

Monday

Deluxe Waldorf Salad

Oooh. This salad, along with the Curried Dill Potato Salad, harks back to the '70s salads of our youth made in Tupperware bowls and eaten at seaside caravan holidays between buckets of periwinkles and kreef (crayfish). Ours has a little contemporary edge, of course.

5 Granny Smith apples, cored and sliced
   into very thin wedges (16 or more slices)
3 tbsp lemon juice
3 celery stalks, sliced
1½ cups seedless grapes, halved
½ cup dates, sliced
1 cup diced cheddar
1 cup roughly chopped pecans, toasted

Dressing
1½ cups plain or Greek yoghurt
2½ cups mayonnaise
¾ cup orange juice
grated zest of one orange

Toss the apple slices with lemon juice as you prepare them. Season lightly with salt and white pepper.

Combine the dressing ingredients and stir. Pour the dressing over the apples and toss to coat.

Working in three batches, lay out the first layer of apples on a serving platter. Top with a third of the remaining ingredients: celery, grapes, dates, cheddar and pecans. Continue to layer apples and then toppings until both mixtures are complete. By working in layers, all the apples get some of the deluxe topping as the salad is served.

Serves 8

Mexican Salsa

When I lived in the States, I fell in love with American-Mexican food – especially the sweet $1 margaritas! And the softest flour tortillas.

6 tomatoes, cut into rough chunks
   or 400g cherry tomatoes, halved
1 medium red onion, finely diced
¼ cup lime juice (freshly squeezed is great
   but you might have to settle for bottled)
3 ripe avocados, cut into chunks
60g fresh coriander (or more if
   you're a "cilantro" fan)
¼ tsp ground cumin
2 tsp salt
½ cup olive oil
1–2 jalapeno peppers, finely diced
   (fresh is best but pickled will do)
2 fresh tortillas cut into 4 x ½ cm strips

Place the tomato and finely diced red onion in a large mixing bowl. Put the lime juice into a smaller bowl. Peel and cut the avocado, putting the chunks into the lime juice as you go so that the chunks do not discolour.

Add the avo and lime juice to the tomatoes and resist tossing the salsa at this point.

Wash, spin and chop the coriander and add to the salsa along with the cumin, salt and olive oil and finely diced jalapeno peppers. Finally add the tortilla strips.

Now, very gently, mix the salsa together with the fewest strokes you can manage, either with your hands or with two wooden spoons. You want all the flavours to become acquainted without the ingredients becoming mush. Be gentle.

Serves 8

Black Rice Sushi Veg Dream Salad

I dreamed this salad one morning just before waking. Yes. The Great Composers and I … dreaming delicious things into being! The star anise and fennel are favourite flavours in the pickling liquor. The vegetables just taste better and better the longer they sit in this bath of flavour. The pickled vegetables are also great on a sandwich with a rich meat (like roasted pork belly or roast chicken). Being a pickle, the vegetable bit of this salad can last a good few days in the fridge. Great for weekends away!

Rice

3 cups cooked black rice

½ cup soya sauce

3 tbsp moskonfyt or honey

3 tbsp sesame oil

3 tbsp rice wine vinegar

1 tbsp pickled ginger

Other stuff

3 tbsp sesame seeds, toasted

Veggies

2 large carrot or 4 smaller ones, peeled and finely julienned

2 fennel bulbs, very finely sliced

8 radishes, finely sliced

4 spring onions, julienned

Pickling

1 cup white wine vinegar

1 cup white wine

½ cup sugar

1 tsp fennel seeds

1 tsp coriander seeds

1 tsp black peppercorns

2 star anise

1 tsp kosher salt

2 garlic cloves

Make a little dressing with the soya sauce, moskonfyt, rice wine vinegar, sesame oil and pickled ginger and toss through the black rice.

Put all the ingredients for the pickling liquid in a saucepan, bring to the boil and remove from the heat.

Place all the finely sliced vegetables into the pickling liquid and let them sit in the delicious liquid for as long as possible to pickle (1 hour minimum). Their flavour will be sublime: liquorishy fresh and clean. Lay out the flavoured black rice on a suitable platter (long and thin would be particularly nice). Sprinkle with the spring onions. Arrange the pickled vegetables on top of the rice and sprinkle generously with the toasted sesame seeds.

Serves 8

Afrika Burn Salad

When my Sweetheart and I went to our first Africa Burn Festival in the Tankwa Karoo, we rode our bikes around, taking in all the installations. We wore festival costume with hats and eyelashes and vintage dresses not squeezed into since the Noughties. We held hands and played like eight-year-olds in the desert, taking in the openness and beauty of place and people. In truth, we did not eat much. There was too much to see and do. When we did eat, it had to be brief, clever, and as fresh as we could get camping for five days in the desert. This is a luscious salad of cunning: tins of beans, pre-made dressing, pre-roasted preserved peppers (I got these from The Kitchen, but you could buy them at a grocery or deli) and very good salami (keeps well without a fridge). It was a grounding salad and its colours were much like the sunsets of our Tankwa adventure.

1 tin cannellini or haricot beans
1 tin chickpeas
1 tin 5-bean salad
1 jar preserved peppers, red and yellow,
   torn into strips
1 small red onion cut into fine slices
400g salami, cut into thicker slices
   and then strips
½ cup best salad olive oil
salt and black pepper to taste
½ cup vinaigrette
2 tbsp red wine vinegar or white balsamic vinegar

If you are not camping in the desert, you might want 30g Italian parsley, roughly chopped or 50g rocket. (I managed to keep rocket fresh in a cooler box for a good while – you see, there's the cunning …)
Open the cans. Drain the beans. Add all the other ingredients. Stir your greens of choice through the salad before serving.
Serves 8

Broccoli Soffriti

I could eat broccoli as a meal almost every night. I love it lightly steamed with any salad dressing or with butter, Maldon salt and black pepper. With anchovies, it is just divine. When we use this dish for parties, people eat embarrassing amounts of it! The Soffriti mixture also works well with asparagus when it is in season.

2kg broccoli (or long-stemmed broccoli)
40g anchovies (a small jar)
1½ tsp crushed garlic cloves
15g fresh rosemary (3 sprigs)
15g fresh thyme, leaves picked
½ cup olive oil
lots of black pepper
2 lemons

Preheat oven to 200°C. Cut up the broccoli carefully into florets, retaining a good amount of stalk. Blanche for 3 minutes in a large pot of boiling water. Drain and submerge in plenty of cold water to arrest the cooking process and retain its marvellous colour. Drain thoroughly and set aside.
With a fork, make a rough paste of the anchovies, the crushed garlic, the picked rosemary and thyme. Add the olive oil.
Toss the blanched broccoli with this mixture as well as a few whole anchovies and lay out the florets on a baking sheet lined with baking paper. Roast in a hot oven (200°C) for 10–15 minutes.
The broccoli should be very fragrant and have slightly roasted (singed) extremities. Arrange on a serving platter and be sure to pour all the bits and juices over the pile of broccoli. Add a good grinding of black pepper. Squeeze the juice of one lemon over the dish and arrange wedges around as garnish.
Serves 8

Hippie Tabbouleh

When I was young, my parents sent me to a little art studio called Mud Pottery Studio on the Main Road for art classes. They suspected (quite rightly) that we were not getting much by way of creative outlet at the quite decent "coloured" government school my brother and I were going to at the time (the mid-70s). It was here, I think, that I was exposed to a bit of the hippie culture of the time … art teachers with shawls and long petticoat skirts, with loose Indian florals and those leather sandals and lots of stuff with mushrooms and brown rice. I was bewitched!

1½ cups lentils

1½ cups bulgar wheat

1 cup olive oil

½ cup lemon juice

2 tsp crushed garlic (4 medium cloves)

1½ tsp salt, black pepper

2 tbsp dried oregano or 30g fresh oregano

30g chopped mint

30g chopped dill

30g roughly chopped Italian parsley

1 small red onion, finely diced

2 red peppers, finely diced

4 stalks of celery, finely diced

To finish

200g Danish feta

1 cup black olives

1 cup toasted walnuts

zest of 1 lemon

Boil the lentils in plenty of boiling water until al dente, about 8–10 minutes. Drain and rinse with cold water to arrest the cooking process.

Boil the bulgar wheat in plenty of boiling water until just done, about 5 minutes. Drain and rinse with cold water.

In a large mixing bowl, mix the bulgar and the lentils and add all the other ingredients except the finishing bits. Mix gently but well with two wooden spoons.

Before serving, top the Tabbouleh with the feta, olives, toasted walnuts and the lemon zest.

Serves 8

The Origins of the Love Sandwich

When I used to run my catering company from my home in Woodstock, there were always people dropping in: friends, suppliers, family, clients collecting their dinner party food. Quite often, people would linger to watch and chat, sometimes even participate. It was a working kitchen. And there was industry. We were in the process of creating something delicious, something good.

Often, I would offer a Love Sandwich. There would be a brief discussion to ascertain my friend's state of mind or heart. What was needed here? A sandwich of solace? A sandwich of inspiration? A sandwich to nurture? A sandwich for grounding? Warm or cold? Crunchy or earthy? Fortunately, we would always have ingredients to hand which could make a sandwich quite exceptional. But the Love that was needed could well be a peanut butter sandwich with fresh seeded bread. Or the plainest, plainest cheddar sandwich on a crispy roll. Or a butter and bovril sandwich with the crusts cut off. Love is all about listening and giving people what they need rather than what we think they should have.

Nowadays at The Kitchen, I have an arsenal of delicious things with which to make a Love Sandwich. Sometimes I may be guilty of giving a bit too much love. Perhaps a little more restraint is in order! Making the Love Sandwich is a privilege that binds me in that moment to its receiver.

This is how to build a Love Sandwich ...

**Remember that any sandwich can
become a Love Sandwich
when it is offered with loving attention
and gentle consideration
always bearing the eaters in mind**

Cut the roll in half but not all the way through. Scoop out the top half of the roll so as to accommodate the filling and to cut out excessive bready-ness.

Spread pesto or your favourite spread on either side of the sandwich. Spread the main filling on the roll (grilled chicken, sliced sausage, rare roast beef, grilled aubergine, bacon, gammon, salami), covering the bottom generously. Next, a drizzle of mayonnaise. Then sliced pickles. You may want to add a favourite relish or mustard or caramelised onion or pickled peppers.

Now the salad component: sliced tomatoes, Salad Dressing (see page 215), and finely sliced red onion. At this point you could add extra avo or Danish feta or crunchy slaw or pickle. Then, with tongs, fit a generous amount of salad leaves into the roll cavity above the filling. You'll need the tongs to fit them in. Fingers just seem ungainly at this point. Now, drizzle a little vinaigrette onto the leaves.

The next critical part of the construction I call The Benediction. The sandwich, which up to now may have been a relatively ordinary one, is about to be transformed! Place the now very full sandwich on the board. With a smooth-ended, long bread knife, gently hold down the filling while you bring the top of the sandwich over, your left hand cupping the sandwich to enclose the filling. Now press down gently with your hand so as to gently introduce all the ingredients in the sandwich to each other. The mayo is greeting the chicken, the tomato and Dressing are becoming acquainted, and the vinaigrette is being absorbed slightly by the bread. I say a little blessing over the sandwich and its eater, sending it on its way to do its good work.

Fusion Potatoes

I am weak for these potatoes. I have no resistance to a warm potato with this wasabi mayo dressing! And the pink and green radish and cucumber garnish are my favourite colours together. When I walk past this salad as it is being made, Lucinda flashes a sharp forbidding glance at me, "Don't do it, K!"

1½kg potatoes, unpeeled
10 tbsp mayonnaise
3 tbsp Chinese wine vinegar
1 tsp sesame oil
2 cloves of garlic, crushed
2 tbsp wasabi paste
juice of 1 lemon
8 spring onions, sliced
6 radishes, finely sliced
10g parsley, thyme or coriander
salt and pepper
1 medium cucumber, shaved into
   ribbons with a peeler
large handful of watercress for garnish

Boil the potatoes in plenty of boiling water until just tender.
Drain and leave in the colander until they are cool enough to handle.
Mix the mayonnaise, Chinese vinegar, sesame oil, garlic, wasabi and lemon juice.
Break the potatoes gently with your fingers into bite-sized pieces.
Stir the wasabi mayo mix gently-gently through the still-warm potatoes and arrange on the platter, layering generously with the finely sliced spring onions, radishes and herbs so that all the potatoes get a bit of all this colour and seasoning.
Once all the potatoes have been layered, garnish with the remaining chopped herbs, ribboned cucumber, radish and watercress.
Serves 8

Honey Mustard Sausages

There really is nothing quite like a warm honey mustard sausage, glistening and sticky. It is Temptation itself.

1½kg top-quality pork bangers
½ cup wholegrain mustard
½ cup runny honey
   (Equal parts grainy mustard and honey)

Line a baking sheet with baking paper. Pour on a drizzle of vegetable oil. Line up the sausages in ranks. Mix together equal parts of grainy mustard and honey. Smother the sausages with the honey mustard mixture.
Bake in a preheated oven at 190°C for 25–35 minutes. You may need to turn them halfway through cooking and baste with the honey mustard glaze to ensure even and perfect colour.
Serves 8

Coronation Chicken

So named because it was prepared for the coronation of Queen Elizabeth II in 1953, this old-fashioned favourite is loved in South Africa too. We add our favourite Dhanya chutney to give it an additional kick.

8 deboned chicken breasts

1½ tbsp grill seasoning

4 tbsp olive oil

½ cup lemon juice

Coronation Sauce

2 onions, peeled and very finely
    chopped or minced

2 tbsp vegetable oil

4 tbsp mild curry powder

1 tsp ground cumin

1 tsp turmeric

½ tsp chilli powder

1 3cm cinnamon stick

5 cardamon pods, crushed

1 bay leaf

4 tsp tomato paste or
    sundried tomato pesto

2 tbsp chutney

2 tsp sugar

juice of 1 juicy lemon

¼ cup chicken stock

¼ cup white wine (optional)

salt and white pepper

⅔ cup mayonnaise

⅔ cup Greek yoghurt

To garnish

¼ cup toasted almonds

10g coriander leaves

Season the prepared breasts with salt and pepper or grill seasoning. Lay them out neatly in a baking tray and drizzle with the oil and lemon juice. Bake at 180°C for 20–30 minutes until cooked. Allow to rest and cool thoroughly before slicing. Lay out on a serving platter, keeping the breast slices together.

Coronation Sauce is a strong curry sauce to which yoghurt and mayonnaise are added. The sauce must be cool before adding these ingredients. Fry the onions in a saucepan over medium heat until cooked and translucent. Add the spices and cook, stirring for a further 2–3 minutes. Add the tomato paste, sugar, stock, wine, salt and pepper and cook, stirring, for another 3 minutes. Allow to cool for a few minutes before adding the mayonnaise and the yoghurt, lemon juice and chutney.

Mix to create a rich smooth sauce.

Pour over the sliced chicken breasts and sprinkle with the toasted almonds and coriander leaves.

Serves 8

Gremolata Potatoes

My mom makes an excellent osso bucco. When I was younger she would have me chop the parsley and the garlic and zest the lemons for the Gremolata sprinkle that would finish off the dish. I just loved this mixture. It was a revelation to me: how that little trio could bring such freshness and lightness to the dish. I've turned my favourite combo into a pesto.

60g curly parsley

1½kg salad potatoes

2 cloves of garlic, crushed

⅓ cup vegetable oil

juice of 1 lemon

1 tsp salt, black pepper

½ cup olive oil

1 tbsp red wine vinegar

sprinkling of pink peppercorns
    for garnish

First, soak the parsley in a deep bowl of water so that all the sandy bits sink to the bottom of the bowl. Give the herbs a bit of a shake in the water and leave for a few minutes.

Meanwhile, peel the potatoes and boil whole in a large pot of water until just tender, about 15–20 minutes.

While the potatoes are boiling, make the pesto. Drain the parsley and spin thoroughly in a salad spinner. (The drier your parsley, the smoother your pesto will be.) Pick the long stalks off the bunch and place the curly bits in the bowl of a food processor together with the garlic. Pulse until the parsley is thoroughly chopped. With the motor running, slowly drizzle in the vegetable oil. Now add the lemon juice and 1 teaspoon of salt and a solid grinding of black pepper. You should have a creamy, bright green pesto.

In a medium-sized bowl, gently break 4 of the potatoes with your fingers into rough bite-sized pieces. In this bowl, splash the potatoes with olive oil and season the potatoes generously with the salt. (Do not be shy. Potatoes need salt.) Sprinkle with red wine vinegar and then 4 tablespoons of the Gremolata pesto. Toss these seasoned potatoes gently with your fingers until they are coated with the pesto. Assemble the potato salad in batches in this way: olive oil, salt, red wine vinegar, Gremolata pesto until all the potatoes are done. This way the potatoes are lovingly and evenly coated.

You may not use up all the pesto but then you have delicious leftovers to put on sandwiches or stir through some fragrant rice.

Serves 8

Beetroot Orange Feta Salad

Let's not mess around: this salad is a great addition to any table. A great one for showing off! You could make a naughty addition of a rose grapefruit. And nowadays you can find beautiful sprouts at markets and supermarkets!

1kg small beetroot

1 red onion

5 oranges

bag of crisp salad leaves

400g Danish feta, broken into larger
    chunks or cubed

150g walnuts or hazelnuts, toasted

30g Italian parsley, roughly chopped

30g sprouts (beetroot sprouts are
    particularly pretty if you can find them)
    or micro greens

Cider Vinaigrette

2 tbsp runny honey

4 tbsp cider vinegar

½ tsp sea salt

½ tsp white pepper

¼ cup olive oil

Boil the beetroot in plenty of boiling water until cooked, about 40–60 minutes. Drain the beetroot in a colander and when they are cool enough to handle, slip off their skins.

While the beetroot is boiling, make the Cider Vinaigrette by whisking the honey, cider vinegar, salt, pepper and olive oil together. Slice the red onion very finely. With a sharp paring knife, remove the rind and all the white pith from the oranges. If you are not in an ardent hurry, you can slice out the segments of the orange and put them in a small bowl. If you are rushing, you can just slice the oranges. Slice the peeled beetroots into bite-sized wedges and toss with a little of the vinaigrette as you go.

Place the salad leaves on a serving platter, delicately tearing larger unmanageable ones with your fingers so that they will be eaten rather than just being decorative. Now arrange the sliced beetroots on top and the sliced oranges between them. Scatter the red onion over the salad and add the feta pieces to the salad. Drizzle the Cider Vinaigrette over the beetroot orange arrangement and, finally, scatter the toasted nuts, roughly chopped parsley and the sprouts.

Serves 8

Cheesecake Squares

Customers have described our cheesecake as a definitive cheesecake. Oh, the hardship of having to sample endless cheesecakes until you find The One!

For the base
140g plain flour (1 cup)
¼ tsp baking powder
50g castor sugar
50g butter
2 egg yolks, slightly beaten

Filling
900g cream cheese
190g castor sugar (rounded ⅔ cup)
1 tsp vanilla essence
4 eggs

Preheat the oven to 150°C.

You will need a 24 x 30cm baking tin lined with baking paper.

You will need another larger tin in which to put this tin when it bakes.

To make the base, put the flour, baking powder, castor sugar and butter in a freestanding mixer with a paddle attachment. Beat until your mixture looks sandy. Add the slightly beaten egg yolk.

The mixture will be stickier but still a bit "sandy". Press this pastry into the prepared tin and flatten with the ball of your hand to make a base. Bake in the preheated oven for 15–20 minutes or until golden brown. Set aside to cool.

For the filling, place the cream cheese, castor sugar and vanilla in a standing mixer with a paddle attachment and beat on a slow speed until you have a very smooth, thick mixture. Add the eggs one at a time while slowly beating, scraping down the sides of the bowl after each egg.

The mixture should be smooth and creamy. Now turn the mixer up higher and beat for 1 minute to make it lighter and creamier. Be careful not to overbeat or the mixture will split.

Pour onto the cooled base. Put the unbaked cheesecake in its tin inside the second deep baking tin. Carefully pour water in the larger tin until it reaches two-thirds of the way up the cake tin.

Bake for 25–30 minutes or until golden brown but still slightly wobbly in the centre. The cheesecake will set more as it cools. Do not be tempted to overcook. Leave the cheesecake to cool slightly in the tin, then cover and refrigerate overnight.

Cut into squares to serve.

Makes 24 squares

Tuesday

TUESDAY

Maroccan Couscous.
Indonesian Rice
South East Asian
Noodles

Kedgeree
Black Bea...
Double C...

Aubs w...

Pickled Cauliflower

This is a great salad for taking away on a weekend. It is great with salami, on sandwiches, anything really …
and it just gets better.

2 cauliflowers
1 large red onion, thinly sliced
1 tsp garlic
¾ cup sultanas
3 tbsp capers
1 tsp chilli flakes
3 tsp caraway seeds
3 tsp fresh oregano, chopped
¾ cup olive oil blend
¾ cup white wine vinegar
½ tsp salt
ground black pepper

Slice the cauliflower in large thin slices. Add the red onion slices. In a shallow bowl, mix the remaining pickle dressing together. Place the cauliflower with the dressing and toss to coat, leaving the cauliflower to pickle for as long as possible in the dressing. Serve garnished with roughly chopped Italian parsley.
Serves 8

Double Courgette Salad

The lemon, herbs and olive oil really sing with these courgettes. The sliced, marinated half of this salad can be made well
ahead of time (these are always great things to know when you are entertaining) and the other half can be done later,
even on a braai or griddle pan. The colours are marvellous and the flavours nutty.

1 cup freshly squeezed lemon juice
finely grated zest of 3 lemons
1½ tsp sea salt
freshly ground black pepper
1 cup extra virgin olive oil
24 small courgettes, thoroughly
   washed, rinsed and wiped dry
80g shaved Parmesan cheese
100g walnuts, toasted
2 tbsp vegetable oil
30g basil
30g mint
10g roughly chopped Itailian Parsley

Start with the marinade. Whisk the lemon juice, zest, salt and black pepper together in a bowl and slowly whisk in the olive oil. Place in a shallower, non-reactive (Pyrex, plastic, enamel) bowl.
Slice two thirds of the courgettes as thinly as possible. A good vegetable peeler could be helpful here. Drop the thinly sliced courgettes directly into the marinade. Cover and leave for at least an hour (if possible). While the courgettes are marinating, line up all the other bits: shave the Parmesan, toast the walnuts.
Slice the remaining third of courgettes in long diagonal slices and toss in a tablespoon or two of vegetable oil and grill on a hot griddle pan for 2–3 minutes on each side. You should have nice, impressive charred griddle lines on your courgettes.
Layer the marinated courgettes with the picked herbs, toasted walnuts and Parmesan and the griddled courgettes. You want a pile of salad with multi textured courgettes rather than a flat lifeless one. Finish off with more Parmesan, herbs and black pepper.
Serves 8

Aubergines with Miso & Sesame

If you buy fresh, happy aubergines, you shouldn't have to salt them. If you are concerned, salt with rough sea salt and allow to stand for 45 minutes. You will then want to pat them dry with paper towel before brushing them with oil and roasting them. Do not be tempted to over-oil them! Moskonfyt is a syrup made from Hanepoort grapes found only in the Cape. It is one of my favourite ingredients. Whenever we go into the country, I drive my Sweetheart crazy by insisting that we stop at every farm stall in the hope of finding a haul of moskonfyt.

3 medium aubergines
¼ cup sunflower oil
2 tsp toasted sesame seeds

Miso Sauce
5 tbsp miso paste
4 tbsp moskonfyt (or honey)
5 tbsp water
4 cm piece of ginger, peeled
   and finely grated

Preheat the oven to 220°C.
Slice the aubergines in half lengthwise and then into even wedges. Brush the wedges with the sunflower oil and place them on a baking- paper-lined baking sheet. Roast in the oven for 15–20 minutes until brown and tender.
While the aubs are roasting, place all the ingredients for the Miso Sauce in a small saucepan and heat for 3 minutes until well combined. Dry toast the sesame seeds in a small pan until fragrant.
Arrange the roasted wedges on a serving platter and drizzle with the Miso Sauce. Sprinkle generously with the sesame seeds.
Serves 8

Chinese Slaw

This is a very simple, clean and crisp slaw. The zingy dressing is a fresh addition, setting off heavier flavours.

1½ white cabbages, finely sliced
5 carrots, peeled and julienned
3 cucumbers, julienned
2 red onions, finely sliced
1 cup finely chopped coriander
1 cup finely chopped fresh mint

Dressing
½ cup rice vinegar
3 tbsp brown sugar
¼ cup brown vinegar
1 tsp sea salt

In a large bowl, mix the cabbage, carrots, cucumber, onion and herbs. In a small bowl, mix the dressing ingredients. Pour the dressing over the slaw and mix together with your hands or two wooden spoons. Heap the slaw onto a serving platter and serve with tongs.
Serves 8

Black Bean Confetti

This salad is like a black bean salsa, just waiting for you to scoop up with a tortilla chip. I think it would make a fresh Mexican-style lunch alongside beautifully sliced avos. Black beans are not easy to find. We often use dried ones that we find in Asian supermarkets.

3 cups black beans soaked, drained
    and well rinsed
2 red and 2 yellow peppers, diced
1 medium white (or red) onion, diced
Juice of 2 limes or 3 tbsp bottled lime juice
4 tablespoons olive oil
1½ teaspoon ground cumin
4 tsp honey
½ tsp cayenne pepper
30g chopped coriander
2 tsp salt, black pepper

Boil the black beans in plenty of water until tender. This could take 45 minutes. Drain in a colander and rinse with cold water. Mix beans, peppers and onion in a large bowl. In a separate, smaller bowl, whisk the remaining ingredients into a vinaigrette. Pour the vinaigrette over the bean mixture, and toss well. Add salt and black pepper to taste.

Serves 8

Moroccan Couscous

It's the dressing of this couscous salad that pulls me in. Cardamom. My favourite aromatic. I love it in Bubbah and in ice cream and, of course, in slow-cooked tagines and curries.

4 aubergines, cut into cubes and roasted
6 red peppers, cut into cubes and roasted
2 tsp salt
splash of olive oil
4 cups (800g) couscous
1½ cups toasted pistachio nuts or almonds
30g coriander leaves
30g mint leaves

Dressing
1 cup lemon juice
1 tbsp finely grated lemon zest
1 cup olive oil
3 tsp crushed garlic
20 cardamom pods, bruised
3 tsp cumin seeds, toasted
1½ tsp turmeric

Roast the aubergine cubes in a hot oven until tender and browned. Roast the cubed peppers until tender and slightly charred.
Bring 1 litre of water to the boil. Add 2 teaspoons salt and a good splash of olive oil. Gradually add the couscous, cover and remove from the heat. Allow to stand for 5 minutes and fluff with a fork.
In a generous bowl, gently toss the roasted vegetables, nuts, herbs and dressing.
Arrange in a pile on a (Moorish) platter and garnish with extra herbs and nuts.

Serves 8

Smoked Snoek Kedgeree

When I first saw kedgeree being made in England, I was a bit taken aback by how much cream was poured into it. Then when I tasted it, all paltry concerns of fat content dissipated. I started scheming about how I would adapt it to a South African setting … and make it even better!

2½ cups jasmine or basmati rice

2 tsp ground turmeric or Malay rice
    seasoning of your choice

2 tsp salt

2 sticks of cinnamon

6 cardamom pods, bruised

6 onions, finely sliced

2 tbsp oil for frying

½ cup favourite chutney (to taste)

400g smoked snoek, deboned

500 ml fresh cream

white pepper

Garnish

30g chopped coriander or Italian parsley

4 hardboiled eggs, quartered

Boil the rice with the turmeric, salt, cinnamon sticks and cardamom pods until just done, about 7–8 minutes. The rice will cook some more and absorb other liquids so you don't want to overdo it at this stage. Drain in a colander.

Meanwhile, cook the onions in oil until translucent and then caramelised, over medium heat for 10–12 minutes.

Stir the onions, smoked snoek, chutney and cream through the rice (aaahhhh!). Place in an ovenproof dish and heat, covered, for 20–30 minutes, at 180°C.

Serve garnished with plenty of parsley or coriander and the boiled egg.

Serves 8

Wedge Salad

Red leather banquettes. Lots of chrome. Ginormous sundaes. Coffee from thick white cups … in truth, our salad is a world away from this sort of diner. We make ours with fried tofu but you've got to know that it is great with maple-drizzled bacon. I loved living in the States: fantastically kind people, and every kind of treat: Big Gulps, Wendy's, sourdough pretzels and whole supermarkets of organic produce!

Croutons

½ ciabatta or sourdough bread,
    torn into chunks

⅓ cup olive oil

1 tsp dried thyme

1 tsp kosher salt

1 tsp white pepper

1 tsp paprika

Blue Cheese Dressing

½ cup crumbled blue cheese, softened

½ cup mayonnaise

¼ cup sour cream or Greek yoghurt

2 tbsp lemon juice

6 tbsp buttermilk

30g chopped chives

½ tsp kosher salt

1½ tsp black pepper

Salad

2 heads of iceberg lettuce

4 large tomatoes

½ cup crumbled blue cheese

1 cup finely sliced red onion

chopped maple-drizzled bacon or fried tofu

croutons

2 tbsp chives,
    or chopped fresh parsley to garnish

Toss the bread chunks with the oil, thyme, salt, pepper and paprika. Toast in a 160°c oven for 10–20 minutes until crisped. You might need to turn the drying croutons during the toasting time to make sure you get overall crispy croutons.

Whisk all ingredients together until mixture is smooth and well mixed. For the optional tofu: 200g tofu, cut into 2cm blocks, coated with corn flour and shallow fried in vegetable oil. Set aside to top the salad. Cut the lettuce into wedges and place on the serving platter.

Mix together all the ingredients for the dressing.

Pour a generous amount of dressing over the lettuce. Cut the tomato into wedges and distribute evenly between the wedges. Sprinkle the blue cheese over this and add the slivered red onion, bacon or tofu, and croutons. Garnish with chives or parsley.

Serves 8

Indonesian Rice

½ cup brown health rice

1 cup basmati or jasmine rice

1 cup black rice

Dressing

½ cup peanut or vegetable oil

4 tbsp sesame oil

¾ cup orange juice

2 medium cloves garlic, minced

1½ tsp salt

2 tbsp soy sauce

½ tsp dried chilli flakes

2 tbsp rice or cider vinegar

1 cup chopped fresh pineapple

The Bits

4 spring onions, sliced finely on the diagonal

2 stalks celery, finely sliced

1–2 red peppers, finely sliced

200g fresh bean sprouts

¾ cup raisins or sultanas

1 cup coarsely chopped roasted peanuts

3 tbsp toasted sesame seeds

blanched mange touts for garnish (optional)

Boil all three types of rice separately in plenty of boiling water. The basmati will take 8–10 minutes and the others more like 20–30 minutes. Watch and top up with water to be sure the grains don't stick together. When they are done, drain each pot of rice in a colander and rinse briefly with cold water.

Combine the dressing ingredients in a large deep bowl. Add the still-warm rice and toss to combine. Taste. You might want to add more salt or pepper.

When the rice mixture has cooled, add all the other ingredients and toss lightly to combine.

Garnish with blanched mange touts.

Serves 8

South East Asian Glass Noodles

There are such clean irresistible flavours in this salad and it is so easy to make. You could add some barely blanched sugar snaps or mange touts for more green or even some roasted peanuts if you'd prefer. In Vietnam, I'm told, meals are served with bunches of fresh herbs arranged on the table so that you can readily pick herbs that you need to add to your meal. What a sensational idea!

400g glass noodles, soaked

½ cup lime juice

½ cup fish sauce

1 small red chilli, thinly sliced

4 tbsp castor sugar

4 cloves of garlic, finely chopped

5 cm piece of ginger, peeled and
    finely julienned

½ cup finely chopped coriander stalks
    (and some leaves too)

4 tbsp sesame oil

1 large green pawpaw or papaya or green
    melon, peeled, seeded and thinly sliced

4 celery stalks,
    very thinly sliced on the diagonal

coriander leaves

Put the glass noodles into a bowl and pour over boiling water to cover. When the noodles are transparent, drain and pour some cold water over the noodles while they are in a colander. Pour the cooled, drained noodles onto a salad platter.

Put the lime juice, fish sauce, sliced chilli, castor sugar, garlic, julienned ginger and coriander stalks into a bowl and mix until the sugar has dissolved. Add the sesame oil, papaya or melon and celery and mix well.

Arrange the salad on top of the noodles and mix through briefly so that the noodles get all the great nam chouc-like dressing.

Sprinkle with the coriander leaves.

Serves 8

Florentine Bites

We know that most people don't need a large slice of cake after lunch and so we craft the most perfect bite-sized treats for an ending. Being a one-bite morsel, the stakes are high: it has to be a bite of perfection – quintessentially chocolatey or lemony, creamy or nutty.

200g excellent-quality dark chocolate

2½ cups cornflakes

50g sultanas or cranberries

1 cup flaked almonds, toasted

115g (½ cup) glacé cherries

25g (¼ cup) glacé ginger

50g (⅓ cup) cut mixed peel

1 cup sweetened condensed milk

Preheat oven to 180°C.

Line the base of a shallow 20 cm square cake tin with baking paper. Lightly grease the sides.

Melt the chocolate in a heatproof bowl set over a pan of hot water.

Spread the melted chocolate evenly over the base of the tin.

Put in the fridge to set.

Place the cornflakes, sultanas, almonds, glacé fruit and mixed peel in a large bowl. Pour over the condensed milk and toss the mixture gently, using a fork.

Spread the mixture evenly over the chocolate base and bake for 12–15 minutes.

Leave to cool before cutting into tiny squares with a very sharp knife.

Makes 30 small bites

Wednesday

Breyani Rice

Real breyani for me has always belonged to the realms of the Breyani Queens, revered matrons who rule the domain. There are a few aspirant princes too who use their breyani to woo lovelies. It is a dish that demands time and attention and considerable commitment. Our breyani has much of the delicious element but is more of a warm salad that escapes some of the rigours of the purist.

2 cups of pre-seasoned breyani rice
    (it looks yellow and contains
    all the spices below)
6 onions, finely sliced
6 carrots julienned
250g frozen peas
60g coriander, roughly chopped
½ cup dhanya chutney or
    chutney of your choice
1½ cups of plain yoghurt seasoned with
salt, pepper and 2 tsp garam masala
5 hardboiled eggs, quartered

*If you can't buy ready seasoned
    breyani rice, make your own:*
2 pieces stick cinnamon
3 cardamom pods, crushed
3 whole cloves
3 all-spice berries
1½ tbsp ground coriander
1 tbsp ground turmeric
2 tsp ground cumin
2 tsp fennel seed
2 tsp chilli powder
4 tsp turmeric
1 cup of lentils
2 tsp salt

Cook the breyani rice, with all the spices, in boiling water till tender, about 14 minutes. Be careful not to overcook the rice. Drain. If you like, you might want to take off some of the cooking spices that have surfaced during cooking.

While the rice is boiling, fry the sliced onions in a little oil until they are golden and slightly caramelised. Remove from the heat. Blanche the carrots in boiling water for 5 minutes. Remove from the water with a slotted spoon and set aside. Add the frozen peas to the carrot water to thaw briefly (2 minutes). Remove these too and set aside.

Season the Breyani Rice with salt and white pepper, add the caramelized onion and half of the chutney and gently stir through to flavour the rice. Now add the carrots and peas, and stir through gently.

Arrange the rice on a platter, drizzle over the remaining chutney, then the masala yoghurt and the roughly chopped coriander. Arrange the quartered eggs on top. You too can now woo.

Serves 8

Gammon

Gammon is a pleasure to serve the whole year through. Slice as thinly as possible with a sharp slicer or carving knife. We glaze our gammons with our honey mustard mix but you could experiment with any sweet sticky business: mustard and marmalade, cranberry, sticky brown sugar and English mustard.

1 gammon, about 2kg
2 onions, cut into quarters
2 carrots, cut in half crosswise
5 all-spice cloves
2 star anise
2 apples, cut into quarters

Glaze
4 tbsp grainy Dijon mustard
4 tbsp runny honey

Cover the gammon with water and add all the ingredients. Boil according to instructions on the package, usually 45 minutes to an hour. Preheat the oven to 180°C.

Remove the gammon from the water and allow to rest. When cool enough to handle, slip the surrounding net off the gammon and then with a sharp knife, slice off the top layer of tough skin, leaving a good slab of fat. Lightly cut lines in the fat to make diamond shapes and coat the gammon with the honey mustard glaze.

Pop in the oven for 10–15 minutes until the gammon has a beautiful bronzed colour.

Serves 8

Puri Potatoes

I am shameless in bookstores. I sit down at the Cookery Books section and feast. One day I came across this recipe based on the Indian street food, Bhel Puri. I was particularly captivated by the use of sev, the Indian chickpea flour "slangetjies", which you can buy all over the Western Cape at most corner cafés. There are all kinds of flavours from chilli to chutney. Some have peanuts. A salad with all kinds of fresh bits: crunchy, sweet, spicy, topped with slangetjies … how could you go wrong?

6 potatoes
¾ cup plain yoghurt
5 tbsp tamarind chutney (or similar)
4 tbsp lemon or lime juice
Sea salt, black pepper
1 cucumber, chopped into 1cm dice
1 red chilli, deseeded and very
   finely chopped (optional)
1½ red onions, finely chopped
150g dried dates, sliced or chopped
leaves from a bunch of coriander
   (about 50g)
100g slangetjies (sev)
160g plain roasted peanuts

Boil the potatoes in a large saucepan in plenty of water. Cook until tender for about 20–30 minutes. Drain and allow to cool before cutting into bite-sized cubes.

In a bowl or deep jug, whisk together yoghurt, chutney and lemon juice and season with salt and pepper. Pour this mixture over the potatoes and stir to coat without making mush of your potatoes. Now begins the exciting layering:

On your chosen platter, start with the tamarind yoghurty potatoes. Next, layer the diced cucumber, then the chopped chilli (if using), the red onion, dates, coriander leaves, sev and peanuts.

Serves 8

Harissa Chickpea Salad

Maurizio, our Italian meats man, told me one day that he loved chickpeas so much he could stand open-mouthed under a shower of them. Chickpea lovers will understand.

400g chickpeas, soaked overnight

1 cup freshly squeezed lemon juice

1½ cups olive oil

1 tbsp crushed garlic

12 courgettes, thoroughly washed
    and dried

3 tbsp Harissa paste

3 tbsp sundried tomato pesto

1½ tbsp paprika

2–3 tsp salt

30g Italian parsley, roughly chopped

30g coriander, roughly chopped

Drain the chickpeas and boil them in plenty of water until tender, about 45 minutes to 1 hour. Drain in a colander.

While the chickpeas are boiling, make a little marinade for the courgettes with ¼ cup of the lemon juice, ½ cup olive oil and 1 tablespoon crushed garlic. Make ribbons of courgette with a vegetable peeler and drop the ribbons into the marinade.

Mix the Harissa and sundried tomato pesto together, adding a little olive oil to the paste as you do this to make the paste nice and gloopy. Put the chickpeas in a large mixing bowl and add the salt, the softened Harissa paste, lemon juice, olive oil and paprika and mix together well with a wooden spoon. Add the courgettes with all their juices and the herbs.

Serves 8

Chopped Turkish Salad

Although this salad requires dicing and chopping, it is very rewarding to make. It will bring a burst of colour and freshness to your table.

2 yellow peppers, finely diced

1 red pepper, finely diced

1½ red onions, finely diced

500g cherry tomatoes, cut in half

1 medium cucumber, finely diced

1 clove garlic, finely chopped

30g coriander with the stem,
    roughly chopped

30g parsley with the stem,
    roughly chopped

2 tbsp olive oil

2 tbsp lemon juice

salt and black pepper to taste

Place all the ingredients into a large mixing bowl and mix together with your hands or two wooden spoons. Add salt and pepper to taste. Arrange on a serving platter or in a bowl.

Serves 8

Wholewheat Mushroom Celery Salad

Wholewheat has great texture and takes on flavour well. It can be substituted with barley. It is nutty, poppy and ricey all at the same time. This is a "staatmaker" salad.

2 cups wholewheat
salt and white pepper
1 cup garlic salad dressing
1 bunch of celery, leaves and all
500g button mushrooms
    (or others if you fancy), sliced
1 tbsp red wine vinegar

Boil the wholewheat in a large pot of water for 40–45 minutes until it is cooked but still has a bite. Drain in a colander and rinse with lots of cold water to arrest the cooking process.

In a large mixing bowl season the wholewheat with salt and white pepper. Pour over the cup of garlic salad dressing, along with the red wine vinegar, tossing to coat. Set aside.

Slice the celery into 2mm slices all the way up the stalk. Roughly slice some of the leaves too and keep the nicest ones whole for garnish. Add to the wholewheat.

Slice the mushrooms and add these to the salad. Test and adjust seasoning and arrange on a suitable platter.

Use remaining celery leaves (or rocket or oregano) as garnish.

Serves 8

Beetroot Yoghurt Masala

Is it just me who loves to eat bottled beetroot straight from the jar? Cold with a crisp pickled onion flavour: a bit of a personal beetroot experience … With this beetroot salad we are trying to go for that cool pickling flavour along with the creamy masala yoghurt: a real mix-up of my Cape childhood.

8 medium-sized beetroots
½ cup vinaigrette
½ tsp salt
3 tsp sugar
2 tsp garam masala
¼ cup water
1½ cups Greek yoghurt
1 red onion, finely sliced in rounds
30g coriander or Italian parsley,
    roughly chopped

Boil the beetroots in a generous amount of water until tender. Drain them in a colander. Once they've cooled, you'll find that their skins slip off quite easily (you may want to use some latex gloves for this task!).

With a sharp paring knife or thinner cook's knife, slice the beetroots into 2 mm-thick rounds. Arrange these slices beautifully on a serving platter.

Drizzle with vinaigrette and allow the slightly warm beetroot to marinate for a few minutes (think of the tart vinegary business of bottled beetroot), or covered in the fridge overnight.

Mix the salt, sugar, garam masala and water thoroughly through the yoghurt.

Lay the separated onion slices over the marinated beetroot slices, sprinkle over some of the chopped coriander or parsley, and carefully spread the yoghurt mixture over the slices.

Finish with more roughly chopped herbs.

Serves 8

Gorgonzola Fig Tart

This tart is a big favourite. It is rich and so very impressive-looking. Together with some lightly dressed salad leaves, it makes a perfect lunch.

Pastry

125g (¼ block) soft butter

1¼ cups flour

Custard

4 extra large eggs

2 cups cream

Filling

150g Gorgonzola or creamy blue cheese

150g creamed cheese

50g walnuts, toasted

6 rehydrated sundried tomatoes

2 tbsp honey

2 tbsp grated Parmesan cheese

5 preserved figs, sliced

You'll need a 22cm cake tin with removable bottom.

Preheat the oven to 180°C.

For the pastry, place the butter and the flour in the bowl of the food processor. Pulse a few times to combine and then process until the mixture almost comes together. Do not be tempted to overwork. This will make your pastry tough.

Tip onto a work surface and bring the pastry together with your hands. Press into a baking-paper-lined cake tin to make a homely tart shell coming about 3–4cm up the sides of the tin. Avoid thick chunky corners at the base. You want a nice even shell, about 3mm thick.

Prick the pastry with a fork and blind bake for 8–10 minutes.

Whisk the custard mixture together in a bowl and season with salt and white pepper. Set aside.

In the meanwhile, make the filling by mixing together the Gorgonzola, creamed cheese, toasted walnuts, sundried tomatoes and honey in a small bowl.

Sprinkle the tart base with the Parmesan and then spread the Gorgonzola mixture over the base. Arrange the sliced preserved figs in a pattern on top of the Gorgonzola mixture. Gently pour over the custard so as not to upset your careful arrangement of figs.

Place the tart on a baking sheet (this makes taking it in and out of the oven much easier!) and bake in the oven at 160°C for 35–40 minutes until golden brown and set.

Serves 12–14

Spinach Almond Cranberry Salad

This salad is such a winner because it is so ridiculously easy to do, especially if you have the dressing at hand. It is also the only leafy salad we have in this book. We love leaves but they don't hold well in our display fridge. When we do make leafy salads, we use the best leaves, and a green medley of blanched fine beans, sugar snaps, mange touts, finely sliced red onion and pine nuts.

400g baby spinach
¾ cup flaked almonds, toasted
1 cup dried cranberries

Dressing
2 tbsp sesame seeds, toasted
1 tbsp poppy seeds
½ cup white sugar
2 tsp minced onion
½ tsp paprika
¼ cup white wine vinegar
¼ cup cider vinegar
½ cup sunflower oil

In a medium-sized bowl, whisk together all the dressing ingredients. Tip the baby spinach onto a serving platter. Sprinkle generously with the toasted almonds and cranberries, pulling up the leaves here and there so as not to have a flattened salad.
Just before serving, drizzle the dressing over the leaves. The salad will become tossed as people help themselves.
Serves 8

Scotch Eggs

It makes me smile. I never dreamt that I would have the pleasure of making Scotch Eggs, in my view the mark of a "serious" deli, for so many delighted customers! They are magic: tasty sausage meat around a perfectly cooked egg with a great dollop of good mustard.

4 eggs
350g sausage meat
4 tbsp chopped parsley
2 anchovy fillets, drained and finely chopped
2 tbsp capers, drained and finely chopped
50g smoked ham
salt and white pepper
1 egg, beaten
6 tbsp fresh breadcrumbs or Panko
   (Japanese breadcrumbs)
1½ cups vegetable oil for frying

Boil the eggs for 5–6 minutes (make sure the eggs are at room temperature before boiling). Place in a bowl of cold water to arrest the cooking process. Peel and set aside.
Mix together the sausage meat (we squeeze ours out of top-quality pork bangers), parsley, anchovies, capers and smoked ham, and season with salt and white pepper.
Divide the mixture into 4. Spread out a handful of the mixture on your palm in a flat disc. Place the boiled egg in the centre of this mixture and carefully close the meat around it. Repeat with the remaining mixture and eggs. Brush with the beaten egg and roll in the breadcrumbs.
Heat the oil in a wok (we find woks perfect for deep frying) and fry for 6–7 minutes until golden brown. Remove with a large slotted spoon and drain on kitchen paper.
Cut in half with a sharp knife and serve with your favourite mustard.
Makes 8 halves

Crisp Clear Coleslaw

This coleslaw has the sweet virtue of a great summer day!
"i thank You God for most this amazing day: for the leaping greenly spirits of trees and a blue true dream of sky;
and for everything which is natural which is infinite which is yes."
– e.e. cummings

½ white cabbage, very finely shredded
1 small red onion, diced
1 large carrot, peeled and grated
1 stalk celery, finely sliced
3 tbsp organic white sugar
½ cup white vinegar
¼ cup vegetable oil
1½ tsp salt
1½ tsp dry mustard
black pepper to taste

In a large bowl, combine the cabbage, red onion, carrot and celery. Sprinkle with the sugar and mix well.
In a small saucepan, combine the vinegar, oil, salt, dry mustard and pepper. Bring to the boil. Pour the hot dressing over the cabbage and mix well.

Serves 8

Asian Roasted Sweet Potatoes

The Asian lime and sesame flavours in this salad are a great contrast to the rich roasted sweet potatoes. This is an unusual and substantial salad that is delicious with grilled fish. The black beans add a surprising texture. Stir them through the flavoured onion mix so that all the flavours become acquainted with each other.

1½kg red (or orange)
    sweet potatoes cut into chunks
¼ cup sunflower oil
5 red onions, sliced
1½ tsp crushed garlic
1½ tsp cumin seed
¼ cup lime juice
4 tsp sesame oil
2 tbsp fish sauce
¼ cup honey
optional: 250g black beans, soaked
    overnight and boiled until tender
3 spring onions,
    finely sliced on the diagonal
30g coriander, roughly chopped

Toss the sweet potato chunks with the vegetable oil and roast in the hottest oven, spread out evenly on a baking tray, until golden and slightly toasted on the edges. This will take 25–30 minutes.
Fry the onions over medium heat until softened and translucent – about 12 minutes. Then add the garlic, cumin seed, lime juice, sesame oil, fish sauce and honey, and cook a little more to make a nice gloopy sauce. Stir the black beans (if using) through this mixture so that they become acquainted with the sauce. Very gently, using two wooden spoons, stir the onion mixture through the roasted sweet potatoes. Garnish with sliced spring onions and the roughly chopped coriander.

Serves 8

Almond Tarts

When my mom collected me from school, she would often have a treat that she had picked up from a bakery, some treasure that she had discovered. In my young experience, nothing was ordinary. And the shared delight of something pure and good remains with me. This crisp almond tart recalls that simple pleasure.

Short crust pastry
300g plain flour
3 tbsp icing sugar
200g cold butter, chopped
1 egg yolk (from a large egg)
1 tbsp chilled water

Frangipane (almond paste)
125g butter
½ cup castor sugar
1 egg
1 tsp almond essence
1½ cups ground almonds
2 tbsp plain flour
baking paper cut into 1½ x 10cm strips,
    you'll need about 48 of these
jar of good raspberry jam
200g flaked almonds

To make the pastry, place the flour, sugar and butter in a food processor and process until the mixture resembles fine bread crumbs. With the processor's motor running, add the egg yolk and water and process until the mixture comes together and forms a ball. Turn out onto a lightly floured surface, flatten the pastry into a disc shape, wrap in clingfilm and refrigerate for 30 minutes.

Meanwhile, make the Frangipane. In a standing mixer, beat the butter and sugar until pale and creamy. Beat in the egg and the almond essence. Stir in the almonds (leave some to sprinkle on top at the finish) and the flour. Preheat the oven to 180°C.

To assemble, line the muffin tins with crosses of baking paper strips. This cunning ploy will allow you to remove the tartlets painlessly. Using your fingers, make little tart bases in the muffin tins by lining each one with about 1½ tablespoon of the pastry. You do not want your base to be too thick. The pastry should come to about halfway up the cup. The cases should have the free-form appearance of a homemade pastry case!

Prick the pastry in each case with a fork, and blind bake the shells for 10 minutes or until golden. Once the shells have cooled slightly, spread about 1½ teaspoons of jam into each tart shell. Then spread 2 teaspoons of almond paste on top of the jam. Finish with a generous sprinkling of the flaked almonds.

Bake at 180°C for 20–25 minutes and slightly browned on the top. Leave to cool before dusting with icing sugar.

Makes 24 tartlets

Thursday

Lentils with Roasted Aubs, Feta & Basil

I learnt so much in the tiny galley kitchen at Finns on Chelsea Green (just off the Kings Road) in London. I suppose it is here that I gained confidence as a cook. People were taking me seriously! I worked alongside Australians and New Zealanders in my chef's whites, then took those off, donned my lipstick and went off with the food for the party in a taxi cab to waitress the party that I had just made. We made lots of this popular salad. The lentils are flavoured with extra virgin olive oil, so pull out your best!

5 aubergines, cut into 2 cm cubes
1 cup very best extra virgin olive oil
300g lentils
1½ cups blended olive oil
2 tsp salt and generous black pepper
250g Danish feta, cut into cubes
50g fresh basil, snipped

Toss the aubergine cubes in the blended olive oil and spread out on a single layer on a baking-paper-lined baking sheet. Blast roast in the oven for 20–25 minutes until cooked. The aubergines should be soft inside and well coloured on the outside.

Boil the lentils in plenty of water until just done, about 10 minutes. Drain in a colander and rinse with cold water to stop the cooking process.

Place the lentils in a deep serving platter and add the olive oil, salt and black pepper and toss well. Layer the roasted aubergines, feta and all the snipped basil on top of the lentil base.

Serves 8

Raw Beetroot Carrot Ginger Salad

There is something very virtuous about beetroot. It just has to be good for you. You can almost feel all those antioxidants working immediately … The colour and crunch of this salad is intoxicating.

6 medium beetroots
8 carrots (about 8)
½ cup vinaigrette
a thumb of ginger (about 4 cm),
    peeled and finely grated
zest of 1 orange for garnish

Peel and julienne the beetroot. Peel and julienne the carrots on a long diagonal. Stack a few slices of carrot and slice into matchsticks with your favourite thin sharp knife. Similarly with the beetroot, make neat thin slices of beetroot. Stack a few slices and cut into thin matchsticks. In a deep bowl, toss together the julienned vegetables with the vinaigrette and the ginger.

Arrange in your chosen platter and garnish with the orange zest.

Serves 8

YES

OF COURSE
WE DO CATERING
and not just the most amazing ♥ sandwiches
* as says the New York Times *

2 people to 200 people
weddings, openings, launches, birthdays, engagements, company
lunches, private dinners… any event really, we can do, for you.

TAKE A CARD
OR ASK FOR KAREN

Lemon Atchar Potatoes

This salad is proudly Cape! We use Lemon Atchar from the award-winning Quality Pickles in Rylands Estate but you could use your favourite atchar in this salad to great effect!

1.5kg salad potatoes,
    boiled whole till tender
good splash of olive oil
    (about 4 tbsp)
juice and grated zest of 3 lemons
generous salt and white pepper
300g Lemon Atchar
30g coriander, very roughly chopped

Use a large wide bowl for assembling this salad.
Gently break the boiled potatoes with your fingers into bite-sized pieces (the broken pieces allow the potatoes to take on all the flavour of the atchar).
Splash on the olive oil and the lemon juice. Season the potatoes generously with salt and white pepper. Resist tossing at this stage. Finely slice the Lemon Atchar and add the sliced business along with all the rest of the remaining Atchar relish to the potatoes. Now mix gently with your fingers. Lay out half the potatoes carefully on a platter and layer with the chopped coriander and lemon zest. Finish with the remaining half, more coriander and lemon zest.
Serves 8

Gazpacho Salad

"What do you do with the inside of your rolls?" Here's what we do: we tear them into bite sized chunks and toast them slowly to make croutons for various salads. You can omit the croutons in this salad and it will be just as good.

4 cups day-old artisanal bread, torn
    into bite-sized chunks
4 cloves garlic
2 tsp coarse sea salt
1 tsp cumin seeds
¼ cup red wine vinegar, or more to taste
¾ cup extra virgin olive oil
800g firm ripe tomatoes, cut into cubes
1 cucumber, seeded and diced
1 red and 1 yellow pepper, finely diced
¾ cup red onion, finely chopped
1 cup seedless green grapes, cut in half
30g mint or basil

Preheat the oven to 180°C. Toss the torn bread in a little olive oil and arrange in a single layer on a baking sheet and bake until they are golden, about 8–10 minutes. Allow to cool.
Mash the garlic, salt and cumin in a mortar or on a good board and mash them into a paste. Put the mashed garlic and cumin in a mixing jug. Add the vinegar and olive oil and whisk together to make a dressing.
Now to assemble, layer the bread, tomatoes, cucumbers, peppers, onion, grapes and herbs. Drizzle the dressing over the salad.
The salad will become tossed as it is served. The bread will soak up all the delicious dressing.
Serves 8

Rocket Barley Walnut Salad

The wonderful peppery-ness of rocket and toasted nuts make a fantastic dressing for this barley salad – one of our most popular at The Kitchen. For entertaining, it's a goodie: it covers the green, pulse/carb, fresh tomato crunch requirements of a lunch on the deck.

2 cups pearl barley
20 stuffed olives
5 tbsp chopped Italian parsley
200g cherry tomatoes, halved
½ cucumber, halved lengthways,
   seeded and chopped
5 spring onions, finely sliced
3 sticks celery, thinly sliced
50g rocket

Dressing
100g rocket or wild rocket, roughly chopped
2 cloves garlic, crushed
4 tbsp extra virgin olive oil
450 ml plain or Greek yoghurt
zest and juice of 2 lemons
100g toasted walnuts or pecans
Maldon sea salt and freshly ground
   black pepper to taste

Boil the barley for 45 minutes until tender, and drain well.

Put all the dressing ingredients, bar the olive oil, into a food processor and blend until smooth. With the motor running, slowly drizzle in the olive oil. Stir the dressing through the barley and mix well.

Pile the barley on a salad platter and garnish generously with olives, parsley, cherry tomatoes, cucumber, spring onions and celery.

Top with more rocket leaves.

Serves 8

Grilled Fennel Chicken

Remembering my London days of chef's whites and clogs, I have an image of poussin lined up in baking trays being basted by the simple trinity of soya sauce, lemon and honey. The fennel is so fantastically gloopy and fragrant. You could add fennel seed or a bit of Pernod Liqueur if you were feeling particularly gourmet!

8 chicken breasts, deboned, skin on

salt and white pepper

1 cup extra virgin olive oil

¼ cup sunflower oil

2 red peppers, cut into 2cm dice

2 yellow peppers, cut into 2cm dice

4 fennel bulbs, thinly sliced
   (the cross-section "flower" is so beautiful)

8 cloves garlic, sliced

handful of fennel fronds

2 cups soya sauce

⅔ cup freshly squeezed lemon juice

⅔ cup honey

Place the chicken breasts in a roasting tin or ovenproof dish. Pour ¾ cup of olive oil over the breasts to coat. Season the chicken breasts with salt and pepper and put aside.

Toss the cut peppers with ½ cup mix of olive and sunflower oil. Arrange the peppers in a single layer on a baking sheet lined with baking paper. Blast roast the peppers in a hot oven (220°C) for 20–30 minutes until cooked and slightly blackened on the edges. Set these aside for garnish. Turn the oven down to 180°C.

Place the fennel slices and garlic cloves in a deep pan with 1 cup of water and let them steam, covered, over medium heat until softened and the water has evaporated. Remove the lid of the pan. Still over medium heat, add a few glugs of olive oil, some salt and pepper, and allow the fennel and garlic to cook gently until fragrant and softened. Pour the fennel and garlic confit over the chicken with all the juices from the pan.

Arrange the fennel around the edges of the chicken dish so that the chicken breasts are exposed. Pour the soya sauce and lemon juice over the chicken and drizzle the honey over the breasts. Bake, uncovered, at 180°C for 20 minutes. Remove the baking dish from the oven and baste the breasts with the sauce.

Grill for a further 10 minutes.

Arrange the breasts on a platter with the fennel, garlic and peppers all around, and scatter with the roasted peppers and some fennel fronds. Serve with some plain basmati or jasmine rice on the side and lots of watercress.

This recipe is very impressive with a whole organic chicken.

Serves 8

Cheesy Leeks

Between the mebos chutney flavoured dressing and the cheesy leeks, this salad calls to something in my childhood.

1 iceberg lettuce
   (or cos or baby gem), sliced
2 celery sticks, sliced
1 bunch chives, finely snipped
½ cup roasted cashew nuts (optional)
6 leeks, thoroughly washed
torn toasted croutons
300g mild cheese – white cheddar
   or white gouda
1 teaspoon nigella seeds
   (black onion seeds)

Dressing
2 tsp curry powder
6 tbsp mebos chutney
1 cup mayonnaise
2 tbsp cider vinegar
½ tsp sea salt

Whisk together the dressing ingredients and adjust seasonings to your taste. Set aside.

Arrange the lettuce, celery, chives and cashew nuts on a serving platter. Slice the leeks as thinly as you can with a very sharp knife. Add these to the other salad components.

Scatter the toasted croutons over the leek-leaf-herb mixture.

Cut the cheese into 1 cm cubes, toss with the dressing and add to the salad platter.

Toast the nigella seeds in a pan to just release some flavour (about 1 minute) and sprinkle these over your arrangement.

You may want to add a scattering of snipped chives for garnish.

Serves 8

Black Rice with Sesame, Lime & Coriander

Many of our regulars come into the shop and ask me expectantly, "That one with the black rice … do you have it today?" This is THAT salad. You can buy the rice from Asian supermarkets.

3 cups black rice

2 white onions

6 red onions, cut into chunky wedges

2 garlic cloves, crushed

2 tsp cumin seed

¼ cup lime juice

2 tbsp fish sauce

¼ cup honey

4 tsp sesame oil

1½ tsp salt, white pepper

6 spring onions, peeled and sliced
    finely on the diagonal

1 cup pitted dates, chopped

60g fresh coriander, roughly chopped

Boil the black rice in plenty of water until tender, about 40 minutes. Watch during cooking that it does not catch and burn. You might need to add more water. When tender, drain in a colander and rinse with cold water.

While the rice is cooking, sauté the onions in a little oil until they are soft and translucent, about 15 minutes. Add the garlic and cumin seed and cook for a further 3 minutes. Add the lime juice, fish sauce and honey and sesame oil, and sauté for a further 2 minutes.

Remove from the heat and add the warm sauce to the cold rice with 1½ teaspoons salt and a shake of white pepper. Stir through the rice to combine. And set aside to cool.

Finally add the spring onions, dates and roughly chopped coriander.

Serves 8

Slaw Tartar

I can eat whole bowls of this slaw. You can make a fine tartar sauce to serve with grilled fresh fish by mixing all the ingredients besides the cabbage and the vinegar. As an accompaniment to fish, you might want to add the grated zest of 1 lemon too and a few tablespoons of chopped parsley.

¼ cup capers, roughly chopped

¼ cup chopped gherkins, plus
    2 tbsp of the juice

1 tbsp Dijon mustard

2 cups mayonnaise

¾ tsp sea salt

½ tsp freshly ground black pepper

5 tbsp cider vinegar

½ tsp sugar

1 large green cabbage, finely julienned

In a small bowl, mix together all but the julienned cabbage.

In a larger bowl, toss the cabbage with as much of the tartar sauce as you like. Taste to see if you would like to add more salt and pepper.

Serves 8

Sour Cream Ginger Cake

There is something lovely about a plain cake – a simple slice to have with tea or coffee. We are proud of this one. It is unpresupposing and just perfectly gingery.

185g butter
1 cup brown sugar
3 eggs
7 cm piece ginger, finely grated
1½ cups self-raising flour
⅔ cup sour cream or Greek yoghurt
2 tbsp organic granulated sugar

Preheat oven to 170°C.
Cream together the butter and sugar. Add eggs one at a time.
Add the finely grated ginger, blending until the mixture is smooth.
Fold in the flour, mixing well with a spatula.
You could use a 22 cm baking tin and line with butter and baking paper. We like to serve this cake in a long loaf tin, but it works well this way too. Pour the mixture into the tin, then using a spatula, make a slight indentation on top of the cake batter. Pour the sour cream or Greek yoghurt into this indentation and sprinkle with the granulated sugar. Bake for 45–50 minutes until cooked.
When the cake comes out of the oven, sprinkle with a bit of extra organic sugar for a bit of crunch and sparkle.
Serves 8–10

Chocolate Almond Cake

The roughly ground almonds in this cake give it an almost meaty texture. It is superb. You could use toasted hazelnuts instead of the almonds. Unlike the almonds, you will need to rub off the bitter skins of the hazelnuts after toasting.

225g dark chocolate
small hot espresso or 4 tsp instant
   coffee in 3 tbsp boiling water
200g butter (just under a
   ½ block butter)
80g flour (⅔ cup)
1 tsp baking powder
2 tbsp cocoa
5 eggs
225g castor sugar (1 cups)
125g whole almonds, blitzed in the food
   processor to make ground almonds

Chocolate icing
200g chocolate
1 tbsp butter

Preheat the oven 180°C.
Melt the chocolate in a double boiler (bowl over small saucepan of water). Once it has started to melt, add the hot espresso. Cut up the butter into blocks and add to the chocolate coffee mixture. Resist the temptation to stir.
Sift flour, baking powder and cocoa together.
Separate the eggs, dropping whites into the bowl of a standing mixer. Whisk the eggs whites until they are stiff, then quickly but gently fold in the sugar with a large metal spoon.
Remove the chocolate from the heat and stir to dissolve the last of the butter.
Beat the egg yolks in a little bowl, and add to the chocolate butter mixture. Fold this mixture gently into the sweet egg whites.
Fold in the sifted flour and cocoa and then the ground almonds.
You are folding to keep the air in the cake. Once the flour mix and almonds are just combined, stop folding and using a spatula, plop the mixture into a 23–24 cm cake tin, buttered and lined.
Bake for 25 minutes at 180°C.
To make the chocolate icing, melt 200g chocolate and 1 tablespoon of butter in a double boiler and stir together to make a smooth melted chocolate. Pour over the completely cooled cake.
Serves 10–12

Friday

Rocket Broccoli

Such a bright green, this peppery broccoli is verdant deliciousness.

2 heads of broccoli, cut into florets

Dressing
1 tsp garlic, crushed
30g rocket
1 tsp sea salt, black pepper
1 cup extra virgin olive oil
1½ cups Greek yoghurt (optional)
1 lemon cut into wedges

Bring a large saucepan of water to the boil and blanche the broccoli florets. Drain in a colander.
Put garlic, most of the rocket (save a few leaves for garnish), and salt into a food processor and blitz to chop. With the motor running, slowly add the olive oil to make a smooth dressing.
If using the Greek yoghurt, drop the olive oil amount to 2 tablespoons and add the yoghurt to make a smooth dressing in your processor.
Toss the broccoli with the dressing and lay on a serving platter.
Garnish with the rocket leaves and scatter sea salt and lots of freshly ground black pepper. Garnish with lemon wedges.
Serves 8

Mediterranean Lentils

At The Kitchen we have found that we prefer to offer salads that do not contain meat. It opens our options.
It seems that many, like me, enjoy meat as an accompaniment to my salad. This salad can stand alone with any
leftover lamb. I just love these deeply Mediterranean flavours. Use the leaves to scoop up the salad.

3 cups brown lentils
2 cucumbers, coarsely chopped
5 celery sticks, coarsely chopped
2 small red onions, quite finely diced
6 medium tomatoes, coarsely chopped
4 tsp paprika
5 tsp ground cumin
4 tsp ground coriander
½ cup olive oil
¼ cup lemon juice
salt and black pepper
2 medium butter or gem lettuce

Boil the lentils in plenty of water until just done, about 10 minutes. Drain in a colander and rinse with cold water to stop the cooking process.
Gently toss all the ingredients in a large bowl with all the spices, olive oil and lemon juice.
Serve on a platter spooned over or in the lettuce leaves.
Serves 8

Egg-Fried Rice

Close your eyes, eat this rice out of a bowl with chopsticks and you are transported to ancient lands. It could also be the ultimate comfort food.

400g jasmine rice (2 cups)

4 tbsp sunflower oil

1 red onion, finely diced

7 cm ginger, peeled and finely julienned

1 tsp chilli flakes

2 tbsp sesame oil

1 tbsp salt

1½ tbsp brown sugar

6 organic eggs

white pepper to taste

3 spring onions

small amount of chives for garnish

Boil the jasmine rice in plenty of water until al dente, about 9 minutes. Drain and rinse with cold water. Set aside.

Add the vegetable oil to a wok and heat until its surface smokes slightly. Add the red onions and cook until they are golden. Add the julienned ginger and the chilli flakes and fry until the ginger softens, about 4 minutes. Stir in the sesame oil, salt and sugar and cook for another minute. Remove from the heat.

Whisk the eggs together in a bowl. Add a tablespoon of the oil from the cooked onions to a regular frying pan and put the pan onto a medium heat. Pour the egg mixture into the pan and leave to cook for 10 seconds before folding the egg mixture over onto itself with a spatula and making an omelette. Slide the omelette onto a plate and, when it has cooled slightly, slice into strips and set aside.

Place the rice in a large mixing bowl and season with a teaspoon of salt and a shake of white pepper. Add the onion mixture to the rice, along with the sliced spring onions, and stir it gently through the rice using wooden spoons.

Place the egg-fried rice onto a serving platter and add the egg strips. Sprinkle with the snipped chives.

Serves 8

Asian Chickpea Cauliflower Salad

This is a Kylie Kwong-inspired salad that we have adopted to great effect at The Kitchen. The chickpeas take on the robust Chinese flavours and this dish has great depth. Don't hold back on the coriander at the end.

2 cups of dried chickpeas, soaked
   overnight and drained
1½ cauliflowers, cut into florets
¼ cup oil
4 cm ginger, peeled and sliced julienne
3 garlic cloves, crushed
1½ finely sliced chillies
1½ tsp table salt
½ tsp cumin seed
½ tsp coriander seeds
½ tsp fennel seeds
½ tsp chilli flakes
½ tsp Chinese 5-spice
2 tbsp brown sugar or moskonfyt
½ cup tamari
½ cup rice vinegar
¼ cup lemon juice
¼ cup extra virgin olive oil
30g coriander, roughly chopped

In a large pot of boiling water, boil the chickpeas until tender (about 45 minutes). Allow chickpeas to cool in their cooking water, then drain and set aside.

Stir fry the cauliflower in three batches in a hot wok with ⅓ of the oil (each time) until dark golden brown and a bit caramelised on the edges. When all the cauliflower has been fried, add it all to the wok along with the chickpeas, sliced ginger, garlic and chillies. Add the salt and spices and stir fry together until the spices are swirled through the chickpea-cauliflower mixture (2 minutes). Now add the moskonfyt, tamari, rice vinegar and lemon juice. Lastly, add the olive oil and the roughly chopped coriander.

Serves 8

Curried Dill Potatoes

I ate something similar at a baby shower a few years ago and then endeavoured to make my own. The sweetness of the dill marries beautifully with the curry mayonnaise. We sometimes call this "Darts in the Garage" Potato Salad – again a hankering towards favourite South African salads of the late '70s and '80s.

1½kg potatoes
2 cups mayonnaise
2 tsp curry powder
½ tsp cayenne pepper
2 tsp sugar
1 tbsp white wine vinegar or lime juice
60g dill leaves, picked off their stalks
salt and white pepper to taste

Boil the potatoes whole in a large pot of water. Once tender (about 30 minutes), drain and set aside to cool.
Whizz all the remaining ingredients together in a food processor or with a hand blitzer (we call it the zigzigger).
Once the potatoes are cool enough to handle, break them apart gently with your hands into bite-sized pieces. This will make them more receptive to the dressing.
Put the potatoes in a large bowl and season generously with salt and white pepper. Pour the dressing over the waiting potatoes and stir together gently-gently with two wooden spoons.
Garnish with more dill leaves.
Serves 8

Carrot Cumin Slaw

I think this recipe originates from an old Gourmet *magazine. Ahh! The demise of the legendary* Gourmet! *When I got notice of the premature termination of my subscription, the news caused me to sink into a chair with despair. My son, Ben, looked at me in alarm, read the note, sat down beside me, gently stroked my arm and said, "It's OK, Mom."*

1 tbsp cumin seeds
½ red cabbage, very finely sliced
3 carrots, peeled and julienned
1 pineapple, peeled and julienned
salt and pepper
¾ cup vinaigrette

Toast the cumin seeds in a small dry pan until fragrant.
In a large mixing bowl, toss together all the ingredients along with the fragrant cumin.
Serves 8

Barbecued Sesame Chicken

When I was little, my mom used to make a fantastic fried chicken dish called Hong Kong Chicken. Look as I might through the recipe files and books with place markers upon place markers, I cannot find the Hong Kong Chicken! She is very vague about the recipe. I have been forced to create this one, which is really a yearning after another. No one else seems to mind. They all seem perfectly delighted with the Barbecued Sesame Chicken!

9 chicken breasts, deboned
(Kitchen tips, page 217)

Marinade
7 cm finger of ginger, peeled and
finely chopped
2 cloves garlic, finely chopped
¼ tsp Chinese 5-spice
¼ cup brown vinegar
½ cup water
1 cup soya sauce
2/3 cup brown sugar + 3 tbsp
(for sprinkling before grilling)
3 tbsp sesame oil

Whisk all the marinade ingredients together in a bowl or deep jug. Lay out the prepared chicken breasts neatly in a baking tray. Pour over the marinade. Cover and refrigerate for an hour, or overnight if you can.

Take out of the fridge an hour before you intend baking. Preheat the oven to 180°C. Bake for 20 minutes at 180°C. Remove from the oven and put your oven onto grill. Sprinkle the breasts with another 3 tablespoons of brown sugar and grill for 6 minutes or until the breasts have a deep colour.

Be careful not to overdo the chicken breasts. If you are doing fewer at a time, baking time might be a bit less.

Allow to rest for 10 minutes before slicing.

Serves 8

Oyster Mushroom Rice

This rice is so very pleasing. You could do the same trick with lightly stir-fried cabbage or iceberg lettuce. This is personal food: it may not look very beautiful but it tastes spectacular!

2 cups jasmine rice
2 spring onions, finely sliced
on the diagonal
salt and white pepper to taste
3 punnets button mushrooms
2/3 cup oyster sauce
10g chives, snipped

Boil the rice in plenty of water until just done, about 9 minutes. Drain in a colander and rinse briefly to stop the cooking process. Place the rice in a large mixing bowl and add the spring onions and season with salt and white pepper. Spread the rice out on a serving platter.

Slice the mushrooms and fry in 2 or 3 batches in a large frying pan until cooked, about 5 minutes each time. When all the mushrooms are cooked add them all to the pan and pour in the oyster sauce. Fry for a further 2 minutes, stirring to mix. Set aside.

Using a serving spoon, make deep diagonal furrows in the rice. Nestle spoonfuls of the oyster mushroom mix into the furrows so that you have loose "stripes" of mushrooms in the rice.

Sprinkle with the snipped chives.

Serves 8

Bulgar with Roasted Peppers, Dates & Coriander

The peppers give this bulgar wheat salad a great flavour and shine like jewels. You might like it, even if you are not a huge pepper person.

2 cups bulgar wheat
4 red peppers, cut into 1½ cm dice
4 yellow peppers, cut into 1½ cm dice
¼ cup vegetable oil
1½ cups pitted dates, cut into strips
50g coriander, chopped
salt and black pepper

Preheat the oven to 220°C.

Bring a deep pot of water to the boil and boil the bulgar wheat for 9–11 minutes. Drain carefully in a small-holed colander or sieve and rinse with cold water to arrest the cooking process.

Set aside in a colander.

Toss the peppers with ¼ cup oil and spread out on a shallow baking-paper-lined baking tin. Roast the peppers until they have good colour and are slightly blackened in places.

Cut the dates into strips and chop the coriander roughly.

Place the bulgar wheat into a large mixing bowl and season with salt and white pepper. Add the peppers, dates and coriander and combine briefly with two wooden spoons. Arrange on a serving platter.

Serves 8

Fine Bean Salad

A fine bean salad is such a good one to have in your repertoire. Three minutes of blanching and you're there!

400g fine green beans
½ cup vinaigrette
1 small red onion, finely diced
10g Italian parsley or chervil, chopped
2 hard-boiled eggs, roughly chopped
Maldon salt and freshly
   ground black pepper

Have your mustardy vinaigrette ready. Bring a pot of water to the boil. Remove the stalk ends (tails) of the beans and blanche the beans for 4–5 minutes (no more!). Drain in a colander.

Toss the warm beans with the vinaigrette. Arrange the beans on your serving platter. Sprinkle with the finely diced red onion and parsley. Garnish neatly with the chopped egg so as not to entirely cover the pretty beans. Season with sea salt and freshly ground black pepper.

Serves 8

Italian Crudité Salad

I am very proud of this salad. I love crudités but I love them particularly when they are coated in sauce without having to be embarrassed about obsessively dipping and dripping to coat them! In this salad, they are essentially raw but scantily clad.

1 head broccoli
1 head cauliflower
3 fennel bulbs
1 bunch radishes
6 courgettes
1 bunch asparagus

Lemony Anchovy Dressing
1 egg
40g anchovy fillets
Juice and zest of 1 lemon
⅔ cup extra virgin olive oil
2 tsp crushed garlic
black pepper to taste

Thoroughly wash all the vegetables, particularly the courgettes, which tend to have fine sand clinging to them.

Slice the broccoli and cauliflower florets as finely as possible with a sharp paring knife so that you have slices that retain their flower shape. Slice the fennel into the finest slices you can manage.

Slice the radishes too, trying again to show off their beautiful colour and shape. Be gracious with yourself. Slicing these vegetables finely is not easy but you will get the hang of it! Slice the courgettes into long, thin, elegant slices on the diagonal. You could use the asparagus raw. We sometimes blanche it for a minute to show off its great colour and to enhance its sweetness. Slice the asparagus too, into long thin slices showing off its elegant shape.

You will now have layers of beautifully sliced crudités in your bowl. To make the dressing, place the egg, the anchovies and the freshly squeezed lemon juice in the bowl of your processor and pulse to make a paste. With the motor running, slowly drizzle in the olive oil until you have a thick dressing.

Pour the dressing over the crudités and mix carefully to coat.

You want to be able to retain the shape of your carefully sliced work without it turning to mush!

Place the coated vegetables on a beautiful salad platter and garnish with fennel fronds. Season with black pepper.

(For drinks parties, we arrange the sliced vegetables in gently curving rows and put the dressing in a shallow bowl. The pink-and-green arrangement is very appealing.)

Serves 8

ake away
small → R30   -large → R40
add meat +R10   ✸SPECIAL!
add veg/cheese +R5   lunchbox
add chicken +R15   salad +
free range   ?? R15 chicken
              R25   R55

he Love Sandwich
starts at R45
au get:

s, pickles, onions,
Red pesto, parsley pesto
vinaigrette, & love potion

oose:
icken OR pork OR bacon
avo, feta OR aubegine 3

Little Lemon Meringue Tarts

Most people have a benchmark lemon meringue pie: some aunt or kid at school who made a memorable one that everyone used to love. It can be intimidating. Set fears aside and try these. They're smaller and winsome.

Shortcrust Pastry
(recipe from Almond Tarts, page 112)

Lemon Filling
8 egg yolks
2 tins condensed milk
freshly squeezed juice and grated
    zest of 8 juicy lemons

Meringue Topping
6 egg whites
1½ cups castor sugar
1 tsp vanilla essence

Preheat the oven to 180°C.

This recipe is best done when you are not rushed. Do it in two stages: the pastry and filling in one and the meringue topping in another.

Press 1½ tablespoons of the pastry into each muffin tin (lined with baking paper crosses). The pastry should come up to about halfway in each little tin to make a neat and not-too-chunky pastry shell.

Pop in the oven for 10 minutes to partially blind bake the shells.

To make the filling, place the egg yolks, condensed milk, lemon juice and zest into a mixing bowl and whisk until the ingredients are very well combined. The lemon juice will cause the mixture to thicken.

Pour the lemon mixture into the partially blind-baked pastry shells and bake in the preheated oven for 10–15 minutes. If you shake it slightly or touch the mixture with your finger, it should feel firm but still slightly soft. Leave to cool completely on a drying rack, then cover and refrigerate for at least 1 hour or overnight if possible.

For the meringue topping, put the egg whites into the super clean bowl of a stand mixer. (Make sure that both the bowl and mixer have not a bit of grease on them.) Mix with the whisk attachment until frothy. With the whisk whisking, gradually add 2 tablespoons of the sugar at a time, giving the whites time to assimilate the sugar. Once all the sugar has been whisked in, add the vanilla essence and whisk again until stiff peaks form.

Spoon the meringue onto the top of the cold lemon filling, making lovely peaks and swirls with the back of a dessertspoon.

Bake in a preheated 150°C oven for 20 minutes or until the meringue is golden brown and crisp to the touch.

Leave to cool completely before serving.

Makes 24 tartlets

Marinated Seared Leg of Lamb with Chermoula & Pine Nuts

This is a delicious way of making a roast leg of lamb and, frankly, it just works so well for catering purposes (and so for you too!). It does not require being served warm and at the last minute. (Phew!) It really does benefit, though, from being marinated. Being served at room temperature, the leg can be carved extra thin: a very more-ish and desirable way to eat lamb. See how the chermoula and toasted pine nuts enhance the flavour of the meat.

deboned, butterflied leg of lamb
  (about 2½kg)
Chermoula (see page 184)
40g pine nuts, dry toasted in a small pan
(or make your own to taste with a
mixture of salt, white pepper, paprika,
dried mixed herbs, a pinch of sugar
and a pinch of curry powder)

Marinade
3 long sprigs of rosemary, finely chopped
4 cloves garlic, crushed
zest of 2 lemons, juice of 3
1¼ cups extra virgin olive oil

Seasoning
1 tbsp your favourite rub or grill seasoning
1 tbsp vegetable oil

Lay the butterflied leg of lamb in the marinade, making sure the joint gets maximum exposure to the marinade. Cover and refrigerate for 30 hours or more.

Before roasting, be sure to take the marinating lamb out of the marinade, allowing it to come to room temperature – a good hour or two.

Preheat the oven to 200°C.

Heat your largest pan on high heat till it is super-hot. While the pan is heating, season the joint all over and generously with the rub or grill seasoning. Pour 1 tablespoon oil into the pan (it should be smoky hot) and using good kitchen tongs; sear the whole leg, fat side down first. Use the tongs manfully and be sure to sear all of the leg so that you lose minimal juices during roasting.

Place the seared leg, fat side up, onto a baking tray and roast at 200°C for 40–45 minutes. Allow the leg to rest for a good while before carving with a long, thin carving knife into the thinnest slices you can manage. Arrange the slices on a platter and serve with the Chermoula and toasted pine nuts.

Serves 10–12

Chermoula

30g coriander
30g flat-leaf parsley
2 cloves garlic, crushed
2 tbsp lemon juice
1 tsp ground cumin
¼ tsp paprika
¼ tsp chilli flakes
¼ tsp cinnamon
¼ tsp salt
¼ cup extra virgin olive oil

Put all the ingredients except the olive oil in the bowl of a food processor and pulse to chop and combine. With the motor running, slowly drizzle in the olive oil to form a rich thick paste.

Makes 1 cup

Roasted Root Vegetables

What many people don't know is that I have been making food for parties for a very long time and through most of the '90s and all of the Noughties, my Roasted Root Vegetables have been my bread and butter. Go ahead and make lots of these. If you are going to the time and trouble of doing them, you may as well do more than you think you'll need since they will do well the next day too!

8 carrots, peeled
8 parsnips
1 large butternut or ½ pumpkin
3 medium sweet potatoes
½ cup vegetable oil

Roasted Root Vegetables truly glow after roasting. Peel or scrub the carrots, parsnips, butternut or pumpkin and sweet potatoes. Cut the carrots and parsnips into long halves. Cut the butternut or pumpkin and sweet potato in long wedge shapes. Toss the vegetables in oil before laying them out, parade-ground style, on a large flat baking tray. Roast in the hottest preheated oven for 30–40 minutes.

They should look golden, even slightly browned from their intense experience, with a few darker spots but definitely no blondeness. Assembling this dish is like building a "fire" with all your autumnal coloured twigs. Most sticky glazes will work well drizzled over these vegetables. The carrots are particularly good with a mixture of 2 tbsp sweet chilli sauce and 3 tbsp fresh orange juice.

Serves 8

Bulgar with Yoghurt, Mint & Roasted Tomatoes

I created this recipe around a suggestion in Claudia Roden's marvellous book, Arabesque. *That's how recipes happen: the idea of cool yoghurt with bulgar wheat, and lots of mint … but then we adapt and add bits that would make it interesting for South Africans. This salad is such a refreshing one, particularly with lamb or any spicy dish. It is a great foil to the Harissa Chickpeas.*

2 cups bulgar wheat
200g cherry or rosa tomatoes
3 tbsp olive oil
2 tbsp sugar
2 tbsp honey
1½ tsp salt
750g Greek yoghurt
60g mint, finely chopped
3 tsp crushed garlic
½ tsp freshly ground black pepper
100g baby spinach

Boil the bulgar in plenty of water for 5 minutes. For this recipe, the bulgar should be slightly underdone so that it takes on the moisture of the yoghurt. When the bulgar has boiled, drain carefully and rinse with cold water to arrest the cooking process. Use a fine colander because the sneaky bulgar slips through larger-holed colanders.

Place the tomatoes in a single layer on a baking sheet and toss with the olive oil, sugar, honey and a little salt and roast in the oven until the tomatoes are blackened in places and well coloured, about 25 minutes. Set aside to cool.

Mix the yoghurt, mint, garlic, salt and black pepper together with the bulgar wheat. It is great if you can allow this mixture to sit for a few hours, chilling in your fridge.

To serve, spoon the bulgar yoghurt mixture onto a platter. Taste to see if you want to add more salt and pepper or a bit more yoghurt. Place the baby spinach on top of the bulgar salad and the roasted tomatoes on top of that. Sprinkle with the olive oil and serve.

Serves 8

Aubergine "Ratatouille"

Everyone should have a tomato sauce that they could make in their sleep. Mine usually has oregano (I am still eking out the real Greek oregano that Kimon and Dimitri brought from their last visit to Greece), a bay leaf, sugar, some red wine vinegar, Worcester Sauce and Tabasco. Margi makes a wicked version with the addition of Dhanya Chutney. Some like a pinch of cinnamon. For a richer sauce, add a small tin of tomato paste. Reach into the flavours you like best and don't stop until you have found them!

4 tbsp sunflower or olive oil
5 onions, chopped (*"grof, rof en onbeskof"!*)
2 tsp chopped garlic
1½ tsp dried oregano
1 bay leaf
3 x 400g tins whole peeled tomatoes,
    chopped, juice and all
¼ cup sugar or palm sugar
1 tbsp red wine vinegar
salt and pepper to taste
1 tbsp Worcester Sauce
5 shakes of Tabasco
4 medium aubergines, cut into 2 cm dice
½ cup olive oil blend
20g basil, snipped

Heat the oil in a deep sauce-pan; add the onions and cook, stirring, over medium heat until the onions become translucent, about 8–10 minutes. Turn up the heat and allow the onions to colour some more, another 4 minutes. Stir in the garlic, oregano and bay leaf and cook for another 2 minutes. Now add the chopped tomatoes, sugar and the red wine vinegar. Turn the heat down again, put the lid on the pot and allow the sauce to stew and reduce for a while, 10–20 minutes. Stir to be sure it does not stick. Adjust seasoning with salt and pepper, Worcester Sauce and Tabasco. You might want it to be sweeter (sugar) or sharper (vinegar or lemon juice) or fresher (good amount of chopped parsley or dill).

While the tomato sauce is cooking, roast the aubs (you could do other classic ratatouille vegetables too). In a large mixing bowl toss the aubs with the oil and spread out in a single layer, with no overlapping, on a large baking sheet. Roast in the hottest oven you can muster, 200°C+ and blast roast for 20–30 minutes until the aubergines are soft inside, have great colour and slightly frazzled edges.

Pour the tomato sauce into a serving dish. Place the aubs in the sauce and garnish the whole dish generously with snipped basil or the herb of your choice.

Serves 8

Koshieri Rice

This rice has its origins in Egypt and there are variations of it all over the Middle East. Perfumed with cinnamon and nutmeg and with much-loved frazzled onions, it could be one of my favourite dishes. Eating it feels like a homecoming. I do like it when people think that I am Levantine. We use Mr Sunshine Vermicelli Noodles. The box is such a happy portent of the deliciousness to come!

2 cups basmati or jasmine rice
200g butter
200g vermicelli noodles
2 tbsp fine cinnamon
1 tsp ground nutmeg
2 tbsp good chicken stock powder
1½ cups boiling water
6 onions, frazzled (sliced and fried
    until deeply caramelised)
salt and white pepper
20g fresh dill, roughly chopped

Bring a large pot of water to the boil, and stir in the fragrant rice. Boil for 7–9 minutes until al dente. Be careful to not overcook the rice. Your vigilance will be rewarded. Drain and set aside.

Put the kettle on to boil. In another deep pot, melt the butter over medium heat and add the vermicelli, the cinnamon and the nutmeg. Stir continually with a wooden spoon, till the vermicelli is somewhat toasted with its butter and spices (we call this "scrooi"-ing the vermicelli) – about 5 minutes. Stir in the stock powder and add the boiling water. Put a lid on the pot and switch off the stove and allow the vermicelli to steam and soften.

Place the rice, vermicelli, frazzled onions, salt and pepper in a large mixing bowl and mix together gently (fingers are best in this instance, I think). You could eat the rice straight away or you could heat it, covered, at 180°C for 20 minutes.

Stir the chopped dill in right at the end.

Serves 8

Beetroot Apple Coriander Salad

At Finns on Chelsea Green, just off London's Kings Road, we'd make lots of this salad for very posh ladies who would come and collect delicious English staples for a weekend in the country. The Beetroot Apple Coriander Salad is still one of my favourites! It works so well wherever it goes!

4 medium beetroots, boiled until tender
    and grated
4 medium Granny Smith apples,
    roughly peeled and grated
(equal quantity of beetroot and apple)
½ cup vinaigrette
1 tbsp honey (optional)
50g coriander, chopped
salt and black pepper

Combine all the ingredients together with wooden spoons or salad servers. Be gentle. You don't want to mush your salad. This one needs serving in a deeper bowl.

Serves 8

Royal Potato Salad

Sweet basil has been known as the herb of royalty. Essentially this is a Pesto Potato Salad but it does look regal somehow with its bright green peas and softly boiled eggs.

4 medium eggs
200g frozen baby peas (petit pois)
1½ kg salad potatoes, peeled
30g fresh basil
30g flat-leaf parsley
10g dill (optional)
80g grated Parmesan
3 garlic cloves, crushed
250ml extra virgin olive oil
1 tsp lemon juice
salt and black pepper

In a small pot of water, boil the eggs for 4 minutes and set aside. Bring a large pot of water to the boil and blanche the peas for 1 minute. Remove the peas from the water with a large slotted spoon and refresh with cold water. Set aside in their colander.

Boil the potatoes whole in the pot of water until cooked, about 30–40 minutes.

In a food processor, combine the basil, parsley, dill, lemon juice, Parmesan and garlic and pulse together with the olive oil until you have a rough herby pesto. Pour into a large mixing bowl.

Once the potatoes are cooked, drain them in a large colander. When they are just cool enough to handle, break them gently into bite-sized chunks with your fingers and place them in the bowl with the pesto. Season the potatoes with salt and white pepper and then very gently toss them with the pesto.

Place them on a serving platter and layer with the peas. Slice the soft boiled eggs into halves or quarters and arrange them over the salad. Give the salad a good grinding of black pepper and garnish with extra torn basil leaves and roughly chopped parsley. Give the exposed eggs a sprinkling of sea salt.

Serves 8

Cauliflower, Red Bean & Feta Salad

There are such sophisticated colours and textures in this salad! People are scandalised: "I had no idea you could make cauliflower taste like that." I call the cauliflower caramelising "popcorning".

sunflower oil

2 small or 1 larger head of cauliflower, trimmed, cut into small florets (about 3½ cups)

2 tsp fresh rosemary, chopped

2 tbsp red wine vinegar

1 can kidney beans, drained

2 large heads of Belgian endive, trimmed, halved lengthwise, then thinly sliced crosswise (optional)

½ cup fresh Italian parsley, chopped

1 cup coarsely chopped walnuts, toasted (optional)

½ cup olive oil

1 cup Danish feta cheese, broken into chunks rather than crumbled

juice of 1 lemon

2 tsp sea salt

½ teaspoon ground black pepper

In a hot wok with a little sunflower oil, fry the cauliflower florets until the edges of the florets are dark and caramelised. To do this, you won't want to stir too much. Leave the florets in the wok for 3–4 minutes at a time, stirring again to caramelise more surfaces. When you've gauged your cauliflower to be mostly done, add the rosemary and the red wine vinegar (there will be a satisfying hiss that sounds like an Asian noodle bar).

In a large mixing bowl, mix the still-warm cauliflower with the kidney beans, endive, parsley, walnuts and a good splash of olive oil and toss gently. Arrange the vegetables on a serving platter and dot with the Danish feta. Squeeze over some lemon juice for zing and season the salad with salt and pepper.

Serves 8

Sumac Slaw

Powdered Sumac is a rich red spice from the Mediterranean that has a tart flavour, a bit like the fleshy sour yellow flower stems (suurings) you find in lush grass. Another of our favourite slaws, this one is cool, crisp and tart: a fantastic accompaniment to most Mediterranean dishes and great stuffed in a pita with our falafel, hummus and tzatziki.

1½ white cabbage, very finely sliced

3 red onions, halved and very finely sliced

2 cups of roughly chopped Italian parsley

1½ cups olive oil

2 tbsp Sumac

juice of 3 lemons

salt and black pepper

Mix all the ingredients together in a large mixing bowl with two wooden spoons.

Serves 8

Sesame Yoghurt Cardamom Cake

This is possibly my most favourite cake ever and I am so happy to share it with you. It is delicious served with yoghurt or mascarpone cream and fresh figs.

220g butter

½ cup sugar

8 tbsp honey

zest of 2 lemons, grated

4 eggs, separated

220g flour

1 tsp baking powder

1 tsp baking soda

pinch of salt

220g Greek yoghurt

⅔ cup sultanas

1 tbsp seeds from approximately
    25 cardamom pods

3 tbsp sesame seeds

Syrup

juice of 2 lemons

6 tbsp honey

rind of 1 lemon

Preheat the oven to 180°C.

Beat together the butter, sugar, honey and lemon zest until creamy. Beat in the egg yolks one at a time.

Into a separate bowl, sift the flour, baking powder, baking soda and pinch of salt. Fold in the batter, alternating with the yoghurt. Fold in the sultanas and cardamom seeds. Beat the egg whites until stiff and fold carefully into the mixture.

Pour into a greased tin, 22 cm in diameter, lined with baking paper. Sprinkle generously with sesame seeds.

Bake at 180°C for 65 minutes. Remove from the oven and leave to rest for 10 minutes.

To make the syrup, boil the syrup ingredients together for 5 minutes, stirring to combine. Pour the cooled syrup carefully over the hot cake or pour warm syrup over the cake once it is completely cooled.

Serves 12–14

Kitchen tips

Vinaigrette

It is such a good thing when you find a vinaigrette that you love. It can really be the make or break of a meal.
This vinaigrette is a good basic. You can tweak it until you find the variation that makes you happiest.

1 tbsp Dijon mustard
1 garlic clove, crushed
1 tbsp castor sugar
4 tbsp white wine vinegar
8 tbsp extra virgin olive oil
sea salt
pinch of white pepper

Put all the ingredients in a jar and shake thoroughly.

Salad dressing

Here's another standby. By adding the oil slowly while blending, you achieve a thicker, "creamier" dressing.

⅓ cup red wine vinegar
2 tsp hot English mustard
pinch of salt
pinch of white pepper
¾ cup extra virgin olive oil

Place vinegar, mustard, salt and pepper in a 1-litre container that you can mess in with your hand blender. Blend together, and with the motor running, slowly drizzle in the olive oil to form a dressing.

Mayonnaise

Dispel fear and take on making your own mayonnaise. All you need is your food processor.

2 egg yolks
1 whole egg
1 tbsp English mustard
pinch of salt
pinch of white pepper
4 tbsp white vinegar or fresh lemon juice
2 cups vegetable oil

Combine the egg yolks, whole egg, mustard, salt, pepper and vinegar. With the motor running, drizzle in the oil through the funnel, in a slow, steady stream. You will see it getting thicker and thicker the more oil you add. Once it is all blended, taste to see if you want to add more salt or pepper or a drop more vinegar.
Use a spatula to scrape the mayonnaise into a container.
Cover and refrigerate.
Makes 3 cups

Blanche

You will need
a deep saucepan
a large slotted spoon
a large colander
a scoop of ice

Heat a deep pot of water to a rolling boil with the lid on. Once you start blanching leave the lid off.

While you are waiting for the water to come to the boil, prepare your vegetables. Peel, trim, slice, dice or julienne your vegetables and have them all ready before you start blanching. If you have large amounts of vegetables, you may want to blanche in stages so that the water retains its boil.

The key is readiness and speed. Blanching times could vary from 2 to 5 minutes. The principle is to immerse the vegetables for a very short period of time, so that they are barely cooked but still tender. Then, with large slotted spoon at the ready, remove the vegetables to the colander and immediately spray with cold water to arrest the cooking process. You could throw the ice over the vegetables and then spray so that the shock coldness prevents the vegetables losing colour. Move the vegetables around in the colander ever so gently with your hand so that warmer ones at the bottom get some coldness too.

Prep vegetables

You will need
a sharp sturdy cook's knife (carrots,
    courgettes, cucumbers, papaya)
or a long sharp slicer (cabbage)
or a sharp serrated paring knife
    (apples, beetroot, tomatoes)
a good, generous chopping board
    (small ones are tricky)
a bowl for the compost trimmings
a bowl for prepared vegetables

Peel the vegetables where required (carrots, butternut, pumpkin, potatoes, onions, beetroot).

Julienne describes vegetables cut into matchstick-sized strips. At The Kitchen, julienned vegetables are cut thin (near matchstick size) but nearly double the length of a matchstick.

Let's use carrots as our example: Slice the carrot on the diagonal to the length that you want your julienned vegetable. Now stack a few slices together and with the fingers of your left hand (if you are right-handed) well out of the way (top knuckles tucked in) slice the long discs into matchstick-sized pieces.

For onions: Slice the peeled onion in half lengthwise. Holding the tufted end of the onion firmly on the board, cut the thinnest slices you can manage lengthways all the way through to the board but not all the way through to the tufted end. There will be a little bit left at the tuft. Holding the slices together, and with your knife now parallel to the board, slice the onion through the slices lengthways so that you have long thin slices. To dice, slice down again through both sets of long slices.

Roast vegetables

You will need

a super-hot oven 220°c or more
   (crank it up to its hottest setting)
a flat, baking-paper-lined baking tray
a bowl in which to toss vegetables
just enough oil to coat the vegetables

Different vegetables require different cooking times, so I'm afraid you can't mix them up on the same baking tray. If you have to put them on the same baking tray, you will need to arrange them with their own kind so that you can take the peppers out before the butternut and so on.

Use baking paper on a flat, shallow-sided baking sheet to prevent sticking. A flat baking sheet will give much more exposure than a deep baking dish.

A single layer of vegetables is what you are aiming for and not too much intimacy: give the cut vegetables space for maximum heat exposure. Too much moisture and you'll get stewed instead of roasted vegetables – you need just enough oil to coat and get them going in the oven.

Vegetables roasted with honey or sugar need to be watched carefully since they can easily catch and burn if not monitored closely. Blast roast vegetables for 25–35 minutes until they have deep colour and are slightly blackened in places.

A note on roasted aubergine slices or cubes: toss them with vegetable oil in the same way you would toss any other vegetable to be roasted. Do not be tempted to add more oil even of the aubs have a "dry" appearance. Your aubs will end up being terribly oily if you give in to this temptation.

Debone a chicken breast

We cook chicken breasts deboned but with skin on so that they retain their moisture. It is preferable to slice the cooked chicken breast when it has cooled slightly.

You will need

a very sharp boning knife
kitchen shears
a plastic chopping board preferably
   used for this sole purpose

Place the chicken breast portion on the cutting board. If you examine the breast, you will see the bone and cartilage of the breast bone. There is a rounded end and a pointy end of the breast. Holding the breast firmly with your left hand (if you are right-handed) and starting from the rounded end, begin by easing your sharp knife with small strokes, between the flesh and the bone, keeping the whole knife running parallel along the bone, cutting the breast away. You will reach the bottom of a "V" shape. Turn the breast and continue working down, keeping your knife as close to the bone as possible until the bone is removed from the breast. Toward the tip end of the breast there is cartilage, which you will also want to remove. With your shears, trim excess skin so that you have a neatly trimmed chicken breast with some skin to cover most of its side.

Prep

First, gather all your ingredients together. Read the recipe through a few times to get the gist of how you are going to do it. Start with the things that are going to take the longest amount of time, e.g. boil the chickpeas or lentils and, while you are doing this, prepare the rest of the ingredients. Conserve energy. If you are blanching several vegetables, use the same boiling water (that is why I recommend the oversized slotted spoon) to blanche all the vegetables. Once all the bits are ready, you engage in the art of assembling something beautiful.

Wash & prep herbs

Herbs such as Italian parsley, curly parsley, coriander, and vegetables such as leeks, courgettes and spring onions often carry a huge amount of sand. We fill a sink (in your case, a deep bowl or small bucket) with water and let the herbs soak in the water for a while. The grit on them sinks to the bottom, we drain them in a colander, then spin them in our salad spinners before chopping them. Herbs such as basil need to be handled with great gentleness since they bruise easily. After soaking, drain gently and avoid too much spinning. Sometimes, I just dry the leaves with paper towel. Leeks, particularly, need careful washing. Cut off the fibrous root, take off the outer leaf, then slice them down the middle. Soak and wash them thoroughly in a deep sink, then drain and slice them as required.

Bake

You will need
**a good electric stand mixer such as a
  Kenwood or KitchenAid
a food processor
bowls, wooden spoons, spatulas,
  measuring spoons, sieve
baking paper, baking tins
a kitchen scale**

Again, gather all the ingredients around you before baking. Be sure that the eggs and butter are at room temperature. When a recipe calls for creaming, employ your stand mixer properly and allow the mixture to cream thoroughly before adding eggs. Always sift flour after measuring. Think light and airy thoughts.

Other things ...

We very seldom use metal spoons for cooking. We mix salads with two wooden spoons rather than metal ones. Metal tends to break and bruise the delicate vegetables.
We do not add salt to our boiling water except when cooking pasta and noodles.
We prefer deeper bowls and saucepans that allow you to mix and stir without too much mess.
We have our knives sharpened regularly. This makes a huge difference to the cooking process.
We love our food processor. We use it to make everything from pastry to pesto, vinaigrettes, patés, dressings and mayonnaise.
We love our oversized slotted spoons, especially since we do a lot of blanching.

List of Recipes

Monday

Deluxe Waldorf Salad	20
Mexican Salsa	20
Black Rice Sushi Veg Dream Salad	22
Afrika Burn Salad	24
Broccoli Soffriti	24
Hippie Tabbouleh	25
The Love Sandwich	30
Fusion Potatoes	34
Honey Mustard Sausages	34
Coronation Chicken	38
Gremolata Potatoes	40
Beetroot Orange Feta Salad	41
Cheesecake Squares	46

Tuesday

Pickled Cauliflower	54
Double Courgette Salad	54
Aubergines with Miso & Sesame	56
Chinese Slaw	56
Black Bean Confetti	62
Moroccan Couscous	62
Smoked Snoek Kedgeree	64
Wedge Salad	70
Indonesian Rice	71
South East Asian Glass Noodles	76

Florentine Bites	76

Wednesday

Breyani Rice	86
Gammon	90
Puri Potatoes	90
Harissa Chickpea Salad	96
Chopped Turkish Salad	96
Wholewheat Mushroom Celery Salad	98
Beetroot Yoghurt Masala	98
Gorgonzola Fig Tart	102
Spinach Almond Cranberry Salad	104
Scotch Eggs	104
Crisp Clear Coleslaw	108
Asian Roasted Sweet Potatoes	108
Almond Tarts	112

Thursday

Lentils with Roasted Aubs, Feta & Basil	118
Raw Beetroot Carrot Ginger Salad	118
Lemon Atchar Potatoes	124
Gazpacho Salad	124
Rocket Barley Walnut Salad	128
Grilled Fennel Chicken	134
Cheesy Leeks	135

Black Rice with Sesame,
Lime & Coriander 136

Slaw Tartar 136

Sour Cream Ginger Cake 140

Chocolate Almond Cake 140

Friday

Rocket Broccoli 150

Mediterranean Lentils 150

Egg-Fried Rice 151

Asian Chickpea Cauliflower Salad 152

Curried Dill Potatoes 156

Carrot Cumin Slaw 156

Barbecued Sesame Chicken 158

Oyster Mushroom Rice 158

Bulgar with Roasted Peppers,
Dates & Coriander 164

Fine Bean Salad 164

Italian Crudité Salad 168

Little Lemon Meringue Tarts 172

Sunday

Marinated Seared Leg of Lamb with
Chermoula & Pine Nuts 182

Chermoula 184

Roasted Root Vegetables 184

Bulgar with Yoghurt,
Mint & Roasted Tomatoes 190

Aubergine "Ratatouille" 194

Koshieri Rice 195

Beetroot Apple Coriander Salad 200

Royal Potato Salad 200

Cauliflower, Red Bean & Feta Salad 202

Sumac Slaw 202

Sesame Yoghurt Cardamom Cake 210

Kitchen Tips

Vinaigrette 215

Salad dressing 215

Mayonnaise 215

Blanche 216

Prep vegetables 216

Roast vegetables 217

Debone a chicken breast 217

Prep 218

Wash and prep herbs 218

Bake 218

Other things ... 218

Index of Recipes

A

Afrika Burn Salad	24
Almond Tarts	112
Asian Chickpea Cauliflower Salad	152
Asian Roasted Sweet Potatoes	108
Aubergine "Ratatouille"	194
Aubergines with Miso & Sesame	56

B

Barbecued Sesame Chicken	158
Beetroot Apple Coriander Salad	200
Beetroot Orange Feta Salad	41
Beetroot Yoghurt Masala	98
Black Bean Confetti	62
Black Rice Sushi Veg Dream Salad	22
Black Rice with Sesame, Lime & Coriander	136
Breyani Rice	86
Broccoli Soffriti	24
Bulgar with Roasted Peppers, Dates & Coriander	164
Bulgar with Yoghurt, Mint & Roasted Tomatoes	190

C

Carrot Cumin Slaw	156
Cauliflower, Red Bean & Feta Salad	202
Cheesecake Squares	46
Cheesy Leeks	135
Chermoula	184
Chinese Slaw	56
Chocolate Almond Cake	140
Chopped Turkish Salad	96
Coronation Chicken	38
Crisp Clear Coleslaw	108
Curried Dill Potatoes	156

D

Deluxe Waldorf Salad	20
Double Courgette Salad	54

E

Egg-Fried Rice	151

F

Fine Bean Salad	164
Florentine Bites	76
Fusion Potatoes	34

G

Gammon	90
Gazpacho Salad	124
Gorgonzola Fig Tart	102
Gremolata Potatoes	40
Grilled Fennel Chicken	134

H

Harissa Chickpea Salad	96
Hippie Tabbouleh	25

Honey Mustard Sausages   34

I
Indonesian Rice   71
Italian Crudité Salad   168

K
Koshieri Rice   195

L
Lemon Atchar Potatoes   124
Lentils with Roasted Aubs, Feta & Basil   118
Little Lemon Meringue Tarts   172

M
Marinated Seared Leg of Lamb with
    Chermoula & Pine Nuts   182
Mayonnaise   215
Mediterranean Lentils   150
Mexican Salsa   20
Moroccan Couscous   62

O
Oyster Mushroom Rice   158

P
Pickled Cauliflower   54
Puri Potatoes   90

R
Raw Beetroot Carrot Ginger Salad   118

Roasted Root Vegetables   184
Rocket Barley Walnut Salad   128
Rocket Broccoli   150
Royal Potato Salad   200

S
Salad dressing   215
Scotch Eggs   104
Sesame Yoghurt Cardamom Cake   210
Slaw Tartar   136
Smoked Snoek Kedgeree   64
Sour Cream Ginger Cake   140
South East Asian Glass Noodles   76
Spinach Almond Cranberry Salad   104
Sumac Slaw   202

T
The Love Sandwich   30

V
Vinaigrette   215

W
Wedge Salad   70
Wholewheat Mushroom Celery Salad   98

acknowledgements

I am proud to work with a most superb team in The Kitchen. My thanks to all my girls and to Paul for making our shop such an excellent place to be. To our community of friends – thank you for your loyalty and support. We are devoted to you.

What a joy to embark on the endeavour of this book with my dear friends Roxy and Russel. It's been so much fun ... let's just do a whole lot more!

A special thanks to Bridget Impey of Jacana Media who believed in us from the start, giving us lots of room to create something beautiful.

My biggest warmest thanks go to my Sweetheart, David, and our children Ben and Maggie, who so graciously share me with loads of people. You are my sanctuary and my joy.

Photography : Russel Wasserfall

Art Direction & Design : Roxanne Spears

Styling : Karen Dudley & Roxanne Spears

Type Setting : Ross Campbell

Proof Reader : Sean Fraser

Image Processing : Sarah Kate Schäfer

For Jacana :

Publishing Director : Bridget Impey

Production Manager : Kerrie Barlow

First published in 2012 by Jacana Media (Pty) Ltd
10 Orange Street, Sunnyside,
Auckland Park, 2092, South Africa
+27 11 628 3200, www.jacana.co.za

Second, third and fourth impression 2012
Fifth impression 2013, Sixth impression 2014

Text © 2012 Karen Dudley
Photography © 2012 Russel Wasserfall
Design © 2012 Roxanne Spears
All rights reserved. No part of this book may be reproduced in any form and by any means, electronic or mechanical, including photocopying, without permission in writing from the authors

ISBN 978-1-4314-0337-0

Printed by Craft Print, Singapore
Job No. 002224

See a complete list of Jacana titles at www.jacana.co.za